The Kids' Karate Workbook

The Kids' Karate Workbook

A Take-Home Training Guide
for Young Martial Artists

Didi Goodman
Illustrated by Linda Nikaya

BLUE SNAKE BOOKS
Berkeley, California

Published by Blue Snake Books,
an imprint of North Atlantic Books
P.O. Box 12327
Berkeley, California 94712

Cover art and illustrations by Linda Nikaya
Cover and book design by Brad Greene

Printed in the United States of America

The Kids' Karate Workbook: A Take-Home Training Guide for Young Martial Artists is sponsored by the Society for the Study of Native Arts and Sciences, a nonprofit educational corporation whose goals are to develop an educational and cross-cultural perspective linking various scientific, social, and artistic fields; to nurture a holistic view of arts, sciences, humanities, and healing; and to publish and distribute literature on the relationship of mind, body, and nature.

North Atlantic Books' publications are available through most bookstores. For further information, visit our websites at www.northatlanticbooks.com and www.bluesnakebooks.com or call 800-733-3000.

PLEASE NOTE: The creators and publishers of this book disclaim any liabilities for loss in connection with following any of the practices, exercises, and advice contained herein. To reduce the chance of injury or any other harm, the reader should consult a professional before undertaking this or any other martial arts, movement, meditative arts, health, or exercise program. The instructions and advice printed in this book are not in any way intended as a substitute for medical, mental, or emotional counseling with a licensed physician or healthcare provider.

Library of Congress Cataloging-in-Publication Data

Goodman, Didi.
    The kids' karate workbook: a take-home training guide for young martial artists by Didi Goodman, illustrated by Linda Nikaya.
        p. cm.
    Summary: "A take-home workbook for young students of Karate and Taekwondo, complete with puzzles, tests, and training exercises to do alone or with a friend"—Provided by publisher.
    ISBN 978-1-58394-233-8
    1. Karate—Training. 2. Tae kwon do—Training. I. Nikaya, Linda. II. Title.
    GV1114.3.G66 2009
    796.815'3—dc22
                                                        2009014903

2 3 4 5 6 7 8 9 SHERIDAN 16 15 14 13 12

Acknowledgments

I'd like to thank Ricki Kay, Mal May, and Joe Varady for their detailed reviews of the manuscript at various stages. Grandmaster Quynh Ngo, head of Cuong Nhu Oriental Martial Arts, and Master Lap Hoang both made valuable suggestions (but neither should be held responsible for any errors that might have slipped through). Master John Burns deserves thanks not just for reviewing the manuscript but for having persuaded me to begin teaching children so many years ago. I also want to thank all the children (and their parents) who gave permission for their pictures to be used. Special recognition goes to the kids who put in extra hours posing for photographs, which turned out to be very hard work: Antonio Calbo-Jackson, Joseph Gershony, Morgan Gillis, Isaiah Houston, Folasade Kammen, Natalie Ramos, Campbell Ryder, and Cristian Woroch.

Finally, I'm grateful to Gwen Austin, former director of the Redwood Heights Community Center, without whose tireless efforts the children's program at Redwood Dojo would not have gotten off the ground and thrived, and I might never have conceived, much less written, this book. And thank you, too, to Breht Clark, the current Redwood Heights director, and the City of Oakland Department of Parks and Recreation, for their ongoing support of my program and others that teach the positive values of martial arts to people of all ages.

Table of Contents

A Note to Parents about This Book

Every good, honest martial arts training manual—including, now, this one—begins with some version of the following disclaimer:

> Martial arts cannot be learned from a book. This manual is meant to be used only in conjunction with, and as a supplement to, proper instruction from a qualified martial arts instructor.

If martial arts can't be learned from a book—*and they most definitely cannot*—then why are there so many books? There are many reasons. The "why" of this book is simple: Lots of kids take up training in the martial arts, and they can all benefit from productive ways to stay engaged with their training between classes. Staying engaged helps keep up their motivation to continue. Kids need support from their parents, too, to keep them going to class—but "karate parents" don't always know how to support their "karate kids."

This book is a guide that will help young students review what they learned in class, so they can practice and stay engaged. (Older kids will be able to use the book on their own, but younger kids will need someone to help with all the reading.) It provides enough information to help you know what your children should be practicing, so you can encourage their efforts in positive ways. It includes martial arts fun and games. It provides discussion topics for you and your children, helping everyone to better understand what martial arts training is about.

Martial arts training—at least, the traditional kind reflected in this book—is a *discipline* and an *art form*. In many ways, it has more in common with taking piano lessons than with playing a sport. Like piano lessons, martial arts involve a lot of basics and repetition—not just as a way to improve skills, but also as an essential part of the mental and physical discipline. Like piano students, martial arts students who never practice outside class cannot be expected to progress very far—especially when they attend class only one or two hours per week. Parents instinctively know this where music lessons are concerned, but they don't always realize it applies to martial arts as well.

Like music lessons, martial arts can bring benefits to every part of a child's life. But the benefits only come to those who stick with it and don't drop out. Kids who are making slow progress, either because they aren't practicing or because of too many competing activities, are at greatest risk for dropping out.

On the other hand, students who practice outside of class—and have the firm support and encouragement of their parents—advance more quickly and enjoy their training more. For those kids, the sky's the limit!

The curriculum presented in this book covers beginning-level techniques held in common by many popular karate and karate-like martial art styles, as well as many taekwondo schools. The techniques are organized into lessons that are meant to build upon one another. Keep in mind that your children's school may present material in a different order or in different ways.

There will always be differences among martial art schools and styles. Still, certain things are shared in common, like the fundamentals of good posture, balance, and body usage and many basic stances, blocks, and strikes. Furthermore, all traditional martial arts share the essential principles of courtesy, respect, and discipline that are emphasized in this book.

Even within a single martial art style, instructors will differ in how they teach. It's important that you and your children should heed this basic rule:

Always respect your instructor, and follow his or her instructions first.

If the instructor wants your children to learn techniques in a different order, call them by different names, perform them differently, or emphasize different principles, that's what they should do! If it's helpful, encourage your children to write notes about these differences in the margin of the book.

When you encourage your children to practice at home, please use a light touch. The key word should be "encourage." Practice should be fun, not frustrating, and it has to leave lots of room for mistakes. Any kind of practice is good practice; it means your child is engaged. Every instructor knows—and you should keep in mind—that it can take a very long time, and a lot of practice, to correct even the smallest mistakes. The important thing is for your children to keep trying and to enjoy trying.

As for critiquing and pushing your children toward higher goals— in martial arts, that's the job of the instructor, not the parent. But if you can't resist wanting to take on that job, there's a simple solution: join the adult class, and start training in martial arts yourself.

There's one vital job, however, that *only* you can do, and that's to reinforce martial arts values at home. You probably already do this, because martial arts values are universal values, like good manners, self-control, responsibility, and seeing things through. When you praise your children for listening well, getting along with others, doing chores without being asked, and completing difficult tasks, you are helping with their martial arts. At the same time, if your children are having trouble controlling their tempers or are getting in fights at school, you should let your instructor know so that he or she can help.

Finally, don't forget that the most important part of martial arts training is the time spent in class, so make it your goal to get your children to every class no matter what. There's simply no substitute for working hard, side by side with other students, under the guidance of a firm but benevolent taskmaster. Class is where all those important lessons are solidified and put to the test—the lessons about courtesy, respect, teamwork, self-discipline, and perseverance.

Good luck in your training.

PART I

Introduction

CHAPTER ONE

What Is Karate?
What Is a Martial Art?

Karate is a kind of Asian *martial art*. A *martial art* is an art that has to do with fighting and self-defense. Asian martial arts developed in the countries of Asia, like China, Japan, Vietnam, Thailand, India, and Korea. You're probably familiar with some martial arts already.

You may have seen kung fu in movies or on TV. If you watched the Olympics, you might have seen judo or taekwondo. Those are different kinds of Asian martial arts. Not all martial arts are Asian. Fencing, wrestling, and boxing are examples of European martial arts. Capoeira is a Brazilian martial art.

Karate is the Japanese word for a martial art that uses powerful kicks, blocks, and strikes with the hands and feet. Nearly everyone has heard the word *karate,* and sometimes we use it to describe almost any martial art with kicks and punches—even ones that didn't come from Japan. For example, taekwondo has sometimes been called Korean karate. Cuong Nhu is a martial art that comes from Vietnam, but it's sometimes called Cuong Nhu karate. Cuong Nhu actually mixes many kinds of martial arts together into one. Kajukenbo is an American karate style that also mixes different martial arts into one. If you want to learn more about some of the different martial arts mentioned here, look on page 175.

Kara "Chinese"

Te "hand"

Empty Hand

The word *karate* has an interesting story. It began in Okinawa, an island that's now part of Japan. In Japanese the word is written with two characters: *kara* and *te*. *Te* means "hand," and *kara-te* originally meant "Chinese hand"; that is, Chinese style hand-to-hand fighting. That's because Okinawan traders used to sail back and forth to China, and they learned a lot about martial arts from the Chinese.

Later, people changed the way the word *karate* was written in Japanese. They used a different *kara*—another character that sounded the same but meant something different. The new *kara-te* meant "empty hand," and that's the term we use today.

Gichin Funakoshi, a very important teacher of karate in Japan in the early twentieth century, wrote a lot about the meaning of "empty hand." Do you think *empty hand* is a good name for this kind of martial art? Why? Think it over. Then read more about it in the box on page 8.

Kara "empty" Te "hand" Do "way"

Funakoshi also emphasized the word *do* (pronounced *doe*). It means "way" or "path." In English we might say "way of life." Funakoshi didn't want students to practice karate just as a sport or as techniques for fighting with each other. Instead he wanted them to practice karate-*do*, which is a discipline and way of life that could help them be better people and better citizens. He believed martial arts could help people improve every part of their lives—at work, school, home, and play. That's what we think, too.

You might have heard the word *dojo*. It's the Japanese name for the "training hall"—the place where you practice the *do,* or *way,* of martial arts.

Dojo

Did you notice the word *taekwondo* also has *do* in it? It's the same *do* Funakoshi talked about, but in Korean. And the training hall where students practice taekwondo is called the *dojang*.

Tae kwon do—"foot and fist way"

When you read and learn all about Asian martial arts, you'll see the word *do* many times.

Differences between Schools and Styles

As we learned earlier, there are lots of different kinds of martial arts. Even within karate, there are many different schools and styles. All the schools and styles share a lot in common, and they also do some things differently from each other.

If you and a friend both practice martial arts, but you study at different schools, you might be able to see some of the differences between styles. Show each other some of what you've learned. You'll probably discover that you've both learned a low block, a high block, and a front kick. But you may find out that your teacher says to do the block or kick one way, and your friend's teacher says to do it a little bit differently.

Which one is right? Which one is best? The answer is that they're both right. They're both best.

Wait a minute! How can they both be best?

An old proverb says, "There are many paths to the top of the mountain, but the view is always the same." Studying a martial art is like trying to get to the top of a mountain, where you'll be able to see what it's like to work hard, try your best, and be the best you can be. But there are lots of different ways to climb the mountain. There are long winding paths, steep zigzag paths—some people even climb straight up the cliffs. There are paths with lots of trees, and other paths with interesting rocks.

People are different from each other. When they look at the mountain and see the different paths, they make different choices. Each one chooses the path that seems best to them. It's the same with martial arts schools and styles. There are many different ways to teach blocks, strikes, and kicks, and many ways to help students get better, stronger, and faster. Every school and style has its own "best ways." So don't worry if you and your friends are learning different things. And don't worry if your teacher wants you to do things differently from what's in this book.

In the end if you stick with it long enough to reach the top of the martial arts mountain, you'll see that it doesn't really matter which path you take to get there. Getting there is the important thing.

Let's get started.

Things to Do
Which Martial Art Do You Practice?

If you aren't sure of the answer, that's okay. Maybe you just joined, and you don't know yet! You can ask your instructor. See if your instructor will help you find the answers to all these questions, and write the answers here.

1. **What is the name of the martial art you practice?**

_____

_____

_____

2. **Does the name have a special meaning?**

(Sometimes the name describes something about the martial art. Sometimes it refers to a place or a person.)

_____

_____

_____

3. **Where (what country or place) does your martial art come from?**

_____

_____

_____

4. **Who is the founder of your school or style?**

(The founder is the person who started it. Sometimes more than one person shares the credit.)

_____

_____

_____

THE EMPTY HAND WAY

Why is karate called the "empty hand way"? One answer is that karate is a way of fighting—or defending yourself—without using weapons. That is, your hands are empty! It's a good answer, but it isn't the only answer.

The *empty* in *empty hand* is also related to a word used in Zen Buddhism, which talks about emptiness and emptying your mind. For Funakoshi and others, martial arts practice was (and is) a very physical kind of Zen meditation.

What does it mean to *empty your mind?* It means you try to get rid of all your expectations, so you can be ready for what-ever happens. It means you practice hard without thinking, so if something happens, you'll be able to react without having to stop and think. If you can do that, you'll be able to stay calm and do the right thing even in a scary situation, like a fight. This ability can help you act honestly and appropriately in *all* areas of your life. (Remember, it's karate-*do*—a way of life.)

The Zen idea of *empty* isn't really about what's in someone's hand. It's about the whole person and their whole attitude—an attitude of being open-minded and ready for anything. It's an idea shared by many traditional martial arts, including ones that train using weapons. It's all about *how* you practice, no matter *what* you practice.

5. How long ago was your martial art founded?
In what year?

_____

_____

_____

6. What will you learn in your martial art? What kinds
of things do you practice every day? What do the
advanced students practice every day?

_____

_____

_____

7. What do you call the place where you practice?

_____

_____

_____

CHAPTER TWO

Are You Ready to Learn a Martial Art?

It's Fun, but It's Also Serious

Learning karate—or any martial art—is fun, but it's also serious. It's different from deciding to play a sport or a game with your friends. In karate or taekwondo class, you're going to be learning kicks, punches, and blocks—things that have to do with self-defense and fighting. Fighting is a serious matter, even if you never mean to *be* in any fights.

If you misuse the kicks and punches you learn in class, you could hurt other people and hurt yourself—either accidentally, or worse yet, on purpose. That's pretty serious, don't you agree?

Your instructor has to decide if it's okay to teach you these things, knowing there are some people who would misuse them and hurt other people. This is a serious question: *is* it okay to teach you kicks and punches?

It's about Being the Best You Can Be

Your teacher knows that learning a martial art isn't really about learning how to fight and hurt other people. It's really about learning how to be the best person you can possibly be. The best person you can be is one who works hard and tries hard and sees things through to the end. It's a person who listens, learns, cooperates, and gets along with others. It's someone who is as strong and healthy as possible. It's a person who can take care of him- or herself and also help and protect others. The best person you can be is someone who will always use martial arts skills to help and not to hurt.

Your teacher knows that when you're practicing karate, you're really practicing all those skills. That's why it's so great for kids to learn martial arts—that is, as long as they aren't the kind of kids who would be mean or careless and use their skills to hurt people.

Are you the right kind of student for the martial arts? Do you want to be the best you can be? How can you show your teacher that it's okay to teach you martial arts?

Following the Rules of Etiquette

The best way to show your teacher that it's okay to teach you is to follow good martial arts etiquette. *Etiquette* means "rules about the right way to act." Martial arts has lots and lots of rules. In fact, there are so many rules, we aren't going to learn all of them in this book. You'll learn most of them from your teacher and from the other students in your school. Sometimes they'll tell you about a rule, and other times you'll have to learn by watching and copying what they do.

These are some rules you should plan to follow no matter what:

1. Always listen to your teacher and follow instructions.

2. Always try your best—and be willing to work hard!

3. Treat all your classmates with respect. Treat each one of them the way you treat your best friend.

4. Come to class on time—and try to come to *every* class, even if you're tired or don't feel like it that day.

5. Come wearing a clean, proper uniform (see Chapter Four for more about this).

Here are two other rules to keep in mind:

• Good martial artists never use their techniques to goof around, show off, or get in fights.

• Good martial artists are on their best behavior both in and out of the training hall.

Ask your teacher and classmates what other rules you should know about. Learn all the rules of your school and follow them—always!

Things to Do

1. What special rules does your school have?

Every school has rules about where to go and how to act when you're in the training hall. Later you'll learn a lot about how to act during class, but there are also rules for before and after class. They might be a little different in each school. Use this space to write down some of your school's rules. If you don't know the answers, ask your teacher.

_____

_____

_____

2. Do you have to remove your shoes when you come in? If so, where should you put them?

_____

_____

_____

3. Is there a changing room for putting on your
uniform? Where should you put your clothing?
Is it okay to leave things in the middle of the floor?

_____

_____

_____

4. What should you do while you're waiting for class
to begin? Is it okay to run around and make noise
when you aren't in class?

_____

_____

_____

5. Is there training equipment in the school? Is it okay
to use it when you aren't in class?

_____

_____

_____

6. Which equipment may you use, and when?

_____

_____

7. **Where should parents, brothers, and sisters sit or stand while they're watching class?**

_____

_____

_____

8. **How should they act? Is it okay for them to talk out loud? (Some schools don't allow _any_ talking.)**

_____

_____

_____

Your family members might not know the dojo or dojang etiquette, so be sure to find out and let them know how they should act when they're at your school.

Use this space to write down other rules for when you aren't in class:

_____

_____

_____

_____

_____

_____

CHAPTER THREE

What Is Respect?

Do you know what the word *respect* means? Respect is a very important part of martial arts. Martial artists show respect for their teacher, their fellow martial artists, themselves, the dojo, and the martial art itself. Even when they're outside the dojo, martial artists show respect for other people and things.

Showing respect means not being thoughtless or rude or destructive. It means treating people (and things) in a polite way, as if you know they're valuable. That includes treating yourself well, too. Sometimes it means recognizing that someone (or something) is important—or powerful—and treating them accordingly. Sometimes it means seeing that someone (or something) should be left alone—and leaving them alone.

A good martial artist knows that everyone deserves to be treated with respect. That includes people you don't know and people you don't like. It's possible to treat anyone and everyone with respect.

Titles of Respect

A title is something you put before a person's name to show respect for their accomplishments or their position. *Doctor* and *professor* are examples of titles. You should address your martial arts instructor with respect for his or her position. Different schools and styles of martial arts may use different titles. Some schools simply use *sir* and *ma'am.* Others use a term meaning "teacher," for example, *sensei* in Japanese or *sabumnim* in Korean.

Sometimes there is a special term to use when addressing senior students (those who have been practicing longer than you). For example, in a Japanese dojo you might call them *sempai.* There might also be a special name that's used only for the head instructor, with a different term for assistant instructors.

There's a lot to find out. Make sure you learn the right way to address your instructor, assistant instructors, and senior students. If you aren't sure about something, ask! There's room at the end of this chapter to write down the answers. Then be certain you always address people with the proper title of respect.

Bowing to Show Respect

In the karate dojo or taekwondo dojang another way we show respect is by bowing. Here are some of the times to bow, according to good martial arts etiquette:

- Bow when you enter the training hall. Step inside the door and bow toward the room.

- Bow to the teacher when you line up to begin class. The teacher will lead you in this, and you'll bow to each other. You'll also do this at the end of class.

- Whenever you work with a partner, bow to each other before and after practicing.

- Bow to the training hall before leaving: Near the door, turn and face toward the room, bow, then turn and walk out the door.

There are other times to bow, too, and you'll learn them as you go along.

When you first start out, sometimes it feels funny to bow. Maybe you've never done it before. For some kids (some adults, too), it especially feels funny to bow to the training hall. The important thing is just to do it, until it starts to feel like the natural thing to do. Remember, you need to show you're serious about being a good martial artist.

It might help to think of it this way: When you bow to the dojo, you're showing respect for what you're there to learn. You're saying that you understand it's a special place where you get to learn special things. It's important to say that and remember it—every time you come to class.

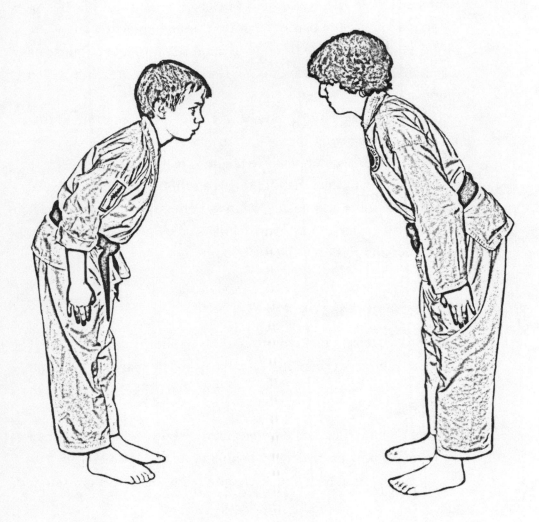

But Why So Much Bowing?

We don't bow very often in our day-to-day lives. It just isn't something we usually do. So when you join a martial arts school and you suddenly have to bow at the door, bow to your teachers, and bow to your classmates, you might wonder what all this bowing is about.

In some Asian cultures, bowing is as common as shaking hands is here in the West. And it has much the same meaning. It's a respectful greeting and a respectful way to part.

So why don't we just shake hands? Because we're following a *tradition*. Asian martial arts have a long history, in which many generations of students have done things a certain way. When we decide to practice these arts, we connect ourselves to that history. The tradition is an important part of what we learn and practice, and we're proud of it. Besides, we think it's a good thing to learn about and experience other cultures. Cultural lessons make our training even more valuable.

But why do we have to do *so much* bowing? Keep in mind that we're practicing *martial* arts, which means arts that have to do with fighting and war. Even though we might be practicing mainly because it's fun, we can't forget that fighting is a serious matter. It can even be a matter of life and death. We must remember that and take it seriously, all the time. Every bow reminds us we must always respect each other and respect what we're doing.

Different Ways to Bow

In most karate and taekwondo schools, students bow with their hands at their sides, bending forward from the waist. Don't bend over too far and keep your eyes up so you can still see the person in front of you.

Keep in mind there are different ways to bow. Your teacher may want you to bow more deeply or hold your hands differently. For example, in Cuong Nhu karate we bow with our hands crossed in front of the chest, showing that our hands are empty (not hiding any weapons).

In some other styles students hold up a fist joined with an open hand.

Your teacher or a fellow student will show you the right way to bow at your school.

Things to Do

1. When to bow.

Can you name at least five different times when you would bow at your dojo or dojang? Write them here:

_____

_____

_____

_____

_____

2. Titles of respect.

In your school, what title is used when addressing your teacher? What about when you speak to a senior student? Does the head instructor have a special title that's different from assistant instructors? Write your answers here:

_____

_____

_____

_____

_____

CONNECT THE ANSWERS GAME: RESPECT

Martial artists show respect at the training hall—and also in everyday life. Draw lines from the numbered people and things on the left to the corresponding letters on the right (or write the letters in the space provided). Some of the answers might work for more than one thing, but see if you can find a way to connect each one to a single best answer.

If you respect:

1. your mom and dad _____
2. your teachers _____
3. your neighbor's dogs _____
4. wild animals _____
5. your toys _____
6. your clothes _____
7. your uniform _____
8. other people's belongings _____
9. your elders _____
10. other kids _____
11. yourself _____
12. tools and equipment _____
13. the environment _____

Then you'll:

a. only use them as they are meant to be used
b. never touch them without asking permission
c. listen to them in class
d. always use good manners with them
e. keep your distance from them
f. always do your best at whatever you do
g. never be mean to them or call them names
h. obey them when they tell you to clean your room
i. never break them on purpose
j. never wear it to play, only to class
k. care for plants and animals, and never litter
l. never tease them from behind the fence
m. fold or hang and put them away neatly

Can you think of other examples of ways you can show respect for people and things? Write them down!

_____

_____

_____

_____

_____

_____

CHAPTER FOUR
The Uniform and Belt

It's important to wear the proper clothes for learning and practicing a martial art. Most martial arts schools have a uniform. In many karate schools students wear a traditional white *do-gi*. In taekwondo schools the uniform is similar (but a little bit different), and it's called *dobok.*

Gi is the Japanese word for "outfit." Do you recognize the word *do?* (If not, go back and look at page 4.) What do you think *do-gi* means? What about *dobok?*

The uniform is the outfit we wear while practicing the *way* of martial arts. When you join a karate school, one of the first things you do is get the uniform you'll be wearing in class. In some schools it must be completely white. Other schools wear black. Some have a school patch that's sewn on the chest or sleeve. Some schools don't let you have any patches or writing on your uniform at all. Others let you put your name or the name of your school on the front or back.

What kind of uniform do students wear at your school? What is it called?

_____

What color is your uniform?

_____

Are there any patches or writing on it?

_____

Why Do We Wear a Uniform?

There are many answers to this question. Here are three:

1. It's *traditional*.

2. It's *practical*.

3. It *sets your practice apart*.

It's *traditional* because Asian martial artists have worn clothes like this to practice in for a very long time. When we put on these special clothes—so different from what we normally wear—we're connecting ourselves to a long tradition, or history. We're making ourselves like the thousands of warriors who have dedicated themselves to the martial arts before us.

It's *practical* because the clothing is loose and sturdy—perfect for working really hard on things, like kicking, jumping, spinning, rolling, and all the other things you might do in class. Your everyday clothes aren't good for this: They might be too tight for you to move freely, or they might tear. That's one reason it's important to change into your uniform before class and not just pull it on over your jeans.

It *sets your practice apart* by saying this is something special, for which you have to wear special clothes. Like bowing when you enter the dojo, your uniform is a reminder that what you're doing is important and serious.

How Do I Put It On?

Maybe you already know how to put on your uniform and tie your belt. Here are some pictures to help you in case you sometimes find the strings and knots confusing.

Let's start with the pants. If you have drawstrings instead of elastic, notice there are one or two "belt loops" (they aren't really for a belt) on the front of the pants and a string on each side. Make sure the loops are in front when you put the pants on. Use both hands to pull the drawstring tight. Always pull on both strings at once—never pull on just one side because you might pull the string out of the other side. Then you won't be able to keep your pants up until you restring them! (And restringing is difficult.)

Once your pants are tight enough around your waist, put both strings through the belt loops in front and tie them together in a bow or a knot.

■ TIPS:

You might want to pull out the drawstring and replace it with elastic. Ask your parents to help you.

Now for the top: Put it on like a jacket. Notice it has four tie strings—one on each front flap of the jacket and one on each side at the hip. Pull the right-hand flap of the jacket across the front of you, and tie it to the string at your left hip.

Now take the left-hand flap of the jacket across the front of you, and tie it to the string at your right hip. Make sure you did the steps in the correct order and the left-hand flap is in front.

■ HINTS:

If your school or style uses a patch on the chest of the uniform, it's almost always on the left side. If you have a patch on your left, check to see if the patch side is on the outside.

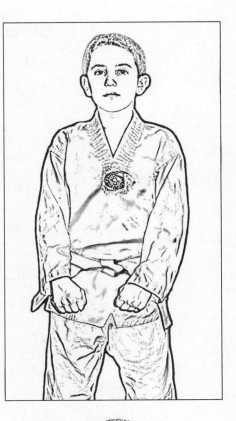

If you wear a taekwondo-style pullover top, skip all the previous steps. Pull it on and you're ready to tie your belt!

The best way to learn to tie your belt is to have someone show you. Practice after they show you. Here are some tips to help after you've been shown. You can also look at the pictures in Appendix A, on page 169.

1. Fold your belt in half to find its midpoint. Start with the belt on your front—not behind your back. Put the midpoint of your belt on the front of your waist, use both hands to wrap the belt around back, then bring both ends back to the front.

2. Tuck one end up under the midpoint of the belt, then tie it all together in a square knot.

3. If the ends of your belt are both pointing down, good job! If one is pointing up and one is pointing down, untie the very last part of the knot and try again.

Should I Wear Anything under My Uniform?

You may wear a T-shirt under your top, if you wish. Please make sure your T-shirt is tucked into your pants, not hanging down below your top.

The pants are designed to be loose and baggy to allow safe, free movement during practice. Wear underpants or shorts under your pants, but please don't wear jeans, sweats, or other pants under your uniform. These restrict your movement and aren't proper martial arts attire.

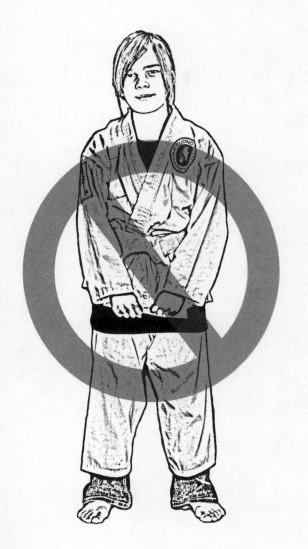

How Do I Take Care of It?

Respect your uniform! Be sure to keep it clean and in good condition. It can be washed just like any other cotton clothes. The belt isn't meant to be washed, so be careful to keep it from getting dirty.

Never wear your uniform except when you're in class—or going to or from class with your parents. Don't wear it when you're playing, eating, or doing anything else besides practicing. When you change clothes after class, fold your uniform neatly and put it in your bag.

Wear your complete uniform and belt to every class. Ask your instructor what you should do if you come to class in the wrong clothing. It's a good idea to do something that shows you know it's important to be in uniform. For example, instead of just joining in wearing your street clothes, ask permission to enter class even though you aren't dressed.

Belt Colors and Ranks

Your uniform came with a white belt. You probably noticed there were other students at the school wearing different-colored belts. Every new student begins with a white belt. Students who come to class and work hard have a chance to earn different-colored belts and sometimes stripes on their belts. Belt colors and stripes tell you something about how long and hard students have practiced and how much they have learned.

Different schools and styles don't always use the same belt colors. Sometimes they use the same colors but in a different order. To know what a belt means, you have to know about the school and style it came from. For example, some schools only use white, green, brown, and black belts. Others use yellow, purple, blue, green, brown, and black. Still others use orange and red along the way. In some styles orange is for beginners, while in others, orange is for more advanced students.

The ranks below black belt are called *kyu* in Japanese, *kup* in Korean. A school may have eight to ten kyu or kup levels (sometimes more). Think of them as steps on the way toward black belt, or *dan* ranks. The dan ranks have different levels, too, which are usually called *degrees:* first-degree black belt, second-degree black belt, all the way up to ninth- or tenth-degree black belt. The highest degrees are for older teachers who have devoted their entire lives to martial arts.

Black belt is a real accomplishment! It takes a lot of work to get there. But anyone can get there, if they stick with it and try their best. You can get there, too.

And after you get your black belt, you don't have to stop. You can still keep learning, practicing, helping others learn, and perhaps earn more black belt degrees. Martial arts is something you can pursue for your whole life.

How Do I Earn Belts and Stripes?

The way to earn stripes and colored belts is to come to class often, work hard, and practice all the things your teacher wants you to learn. That includes following the rules and behaving seriously and respectfully. In short: show your teacher what kind of martial artist you are!

When your teacher believes you're ready for a stripe or belt, he or she will let you know, and you'll take a test. The test will be your chance to show the teacher—and maybe your family and friends—what you have learned. If you pass the test, you'll be promoted and receive a stripe or a new belt.

Don't Think Too Much about Belt Tests!

It's true: You have to take a test to get a new stripe or belt. But that isn't the way you *earn* the stripe or belt. You earn it just by practicing hard and being the best martial artist you can be. If you're always thinking about how soon you get to take a test, you won't be thinking enough about your practice. Your teacher will let you know when you're ready to test, so you don't need to think about it—and it isn't good martial arts etiquette to ask.

Now that you know how it works, forget about stripes and belts and tests, and just get down to practicing like a serious martial artist!

Things to Do

1. The belt race.

This is a race against the clock, but if you're together with friends, you can race each other instead. See how fast you can tie your belt and still have it come out correctly. Can you do it in under ten seconds? Set a stopwatch to count down from ten (or fifteen, if you think you need more time). When time is up, raise both hands in the air! If your belt falls off—you had better try again. Use the pictures on page 169 to check whether you're tying it right.

2. Why do people wear uniforms?

Football players wear uniforms. Why? Nurses wear uniforms. How come? Are their reasons the same or different from each other? Write down some reasons we wear a uniform in martial arts. Are our reasons the same or different from nurses and football players?

_____

_____

_____

3. **What are the belt colors you will be earning in your school? Write or color them in:**

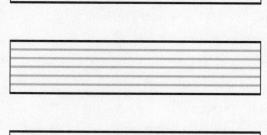

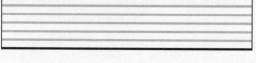

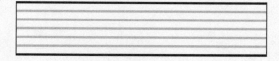

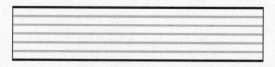

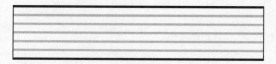

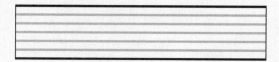

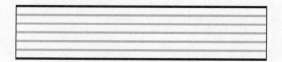

CHAPTER FIVE

Your First Class (and Every Class!)

When you arrive for your first class (or any class), get dressed quickly and wait for the teacher to call *line up!* That's when you'll go to your place in line (according to rank), and the class will bow in together.

Lining Up by Rank

When class is about to begin, all the students will line up in order of rank, facing the teacher. Lining up by rank means lining up in order of belt color, with the most advanced students near the head of the line and the newest students near the end of the line. Not every school does it the same way.

In some schools the most advanced black belts line up in the front row. The next most advanced students fill in behind them, and so on, with the white belts and new students filling in the back row. But in other schools the black belts may line up on one side of the room, with everyone else filling in beside them. Sometimes all the black belts are in front, facing the rows of students. Some schools line up in any order, without regard for rank.

The main thing is to find out where you should be standing in *your* school. On your first day, someone will show you—or if they don't, ask for help from your teacher or a more-experienced student. After that, a good way to find your place in line is to find the other students of the same rank. For example, if you're a new white belt, find the other new white belts and stand with them. If you're a yellow belt, find the other yellow belts and stand with them. Lining up in the right order may sometimes be confusing, but it's always okay to ask for help.

During class you might practice some things in lines; other times your teacher might have you leave the lines to practice with partners, kick the bags or targets, or practice on the mats. Pay attention to where your place was in line, so when the teacher calls *line up* again, you can hurry right back to your place.

The Bowing-in Ceremony

Bowing in is what we call the ceremony that begins every class. You should be able to follow along and learn all the steps in the bowing-in ceremony by doing it with your class. Pay attention and see if you can remember all the steps.

Not every school will *bow in* in exactly the same way, but all schools do it for the same reasons. What do you think those reasons are? Write your answer here:

_____

_____

_____

If you aren't sure, go back to page 18 and read about why martial artists bow. Ask your instructor about it, too. See if your instructor mentions *respect* and *tradition*.

Here is an example of a bowing-in ceremony. As you read this, notice which parts are the same as and which are different from how you do it at your school. Imagine that our example dojo has a flag on the wall, next to some pictures of important old teachers.

- First, the students and instructors turn together and bow toward the flag and pictures. This is a way of respecting and thanking those teachers who have passed down their knowledge. The head instructor calls out *Attention! Bow!* These commands might be in English, Japanese, Korean, or another language.

• Next the teachers face the students, and the commands are called out again. Students and teachers bow to each other to show respect.

• Then everyone stands still quietly for a brief meditation. This is a way to get the mind ready to concentrate on practice.

• The teacher who is leading class indicates when meditation is over, and students return to ready stance.

ATTENTION! BOW!

Japanese (karate): *Ki o tsuke! Rei!*

Korean (taekwondo): *Charyŏt! Kyŏng rye!*

Vietnamese (Cuong Nhu): *Nghiem! Chao!*

Now the workout begins! Pay attention and do your best. Do this for your first class and every class.

At the end of class you'll line up again, and there will be a bowing-out ceremony. Bowing out is similar to bowing in, but it isn't exactly the same. After class try to write down the steps of the bowing-out ceremony and show how it's different from bowing in.

What to Do If You're Late for Class

It's important to be on time for every class. Try your best. But if you're late, it's still okay to come to class; in fact, a good martial artist will come late rather than miss a class.

Please don't just dash into class when you arrive late! Your school will have special etiquette for coming in late. This allows you to

Standing meditation.

show respect for the teachers and class, even though you missed the bowing-in ceremony. It usually goes something like this:

- Stand in ready stance at the side of the room, near the front (ask exactly where if you aren't sure). Watch and wait until the teacher who is leading class sees you.

- When the teacher sees you waiting and turns to face you, you'll bow to each other. Then you may enter and join in the workout.

- Go to your place in line, according to rank. If you have to go across the room, walk *behind* the other students, not in front. (Why do you think we walk *behind?* What if students were practicing kicks or punches when you came to join in?)

The rules might also include something to show that you know it's important to be on time, like doing some push-ups at the side of the room. (Remember when we talked about joining in without your uniform? Same idea!)

What If I Have to Leave Early?

If you know you're going to be picked up early, be sure to let your teachers know ahead of time. Tell them before class, and when the time comes, find them and bow to them before you go. Don't just dash out of class when you see your parents in the doorway. That doesn't show respect. Remember, you'll be missing the bowing-out ceremony, so you must bow out on your own.

What if you have to leave the room suddenly because you feel sick, are hurt, or have to go to the bathroom? Follow this general rule:

> You must have the teacher's permission to leave class for any reason.

If you feel ill or have been injured, the teacher will want to help you and make sure you're okay. That's why you must never leave the room without informing someone. Raise your hand to get permission or get help. If you can't get the teacher's attention, tell a senior student. If you need to go to the bathroom and you can't wait any longer, follow the same guidelines. (And hurry back to class, so you can get right back to work.)

Things to Do

1. What's on the wall?

At your dojo, is there a special place at the front of the room with a flag, a picture, and perhaps other things?

_____

If there's a flag, what sort of flag is it? What does it stand for?

_____

If there are pictures, what do they show? Who are the people in them?

_____

_____

_____

2. Bowing in and out.

What are the steps in your bowing-in ceremony and your bowing-out ceremony? Write them down side by side. How are they the same? How are they different?

_____

_____

_____

_____

_____

_____

3. How do you line up at the start of class?

Write down answers to these four things:

1. Where does the instructor stand?

_____

2. Where do the black belts stand?

_____

3. Where do the beginners stand?

_____

4. Who is usually standing near you in line?

_____

4. What do you do if you're late?

Ask your instructor and write the answer here:

_____

_____

_____

CHAPTER SIX

Warm-ups and Stretching

Every great workout begins with warm-ups and stretching.

Warm-ups get your heart pumping faster and your muscles warm, which makes them ready to stretch and work hard. At the end of warm-ups you should be breathing hard and sweating a little bit (or maybe a lot).

Stretches get your muscles ready for maximum action. If you stretch out carefully (once you're warm), you help your body prepare for the high kicks and hard, fast punches you'll be practicing. The better you prepare for the workout, the less likely you are to hurt yourself while trying to go higher, harder, and faster.

Stretches also make you more flexible. The more flexible you are, the easier it is for you to do things like kick higher, reach longer stances, or bend and turn more quickly.

All these things will help make you a better martial artist.

What's Your Warm-up?

Think back to your class. What exercises happen right after bowing in? That's usually when warm-ups begin. Some classes run laps around the room, jog in place, or do jumping jacks. Some classes play a game of tag to warm up.

Some classes use light, easy kicks and punches to warm up—that is, kicks and punches done softly, without strength or power. Just like jogging in place, this will get you breathing hard and sweating, and it warms up all the same muscles you'll use later, when you practice kicks and punches full speed.

Two Kinds of Stretches

We mentioned two kinds of stretching: stretching to get ready for action and stretching to make yourself more flexible. Some experts believe you don't need to do the first kind as long as you do a good warm-up. Still, there's a strong tradition of stretching before working out, and it feels good to do it.

Stretches to get ready for action don't take very long. Holding each one for a count of eight will be enough for most people. You might also repeat each stretch once or twice.

Stretching to increase flexibility takes more time. If you want your stretches to make you more flexible than you already are, you must hold each stretch at its farthest point for twenty or thirty seconds—*and* you must repeat it a few times, every time you stretch.

Think about it: If you did all your stretches the second way—holding each one for thirty seconds and repeating each one three times—it would take up a lot of class time! There's so much learning and practicing to do in class that your teacher might not want to spend that time on stretching. Stretching to increase flexibility is important, but you can do a lot of it before and after class or at home. A lot of teachers ask their students to come early, stay late, or practice at home to increase their flexibility.

Classes that do include long, slow stretches often put them at the end of practice, when everyone's muscles are very warm from working hard. That's when your muscles are most ready to stretch. Doing long stretches at the end of class also lets everyone cool off and catch their breath before bowing out.

If your class doesn't have time for long, slow stretches, ask your teacher what stretches you should do at home. Get help to make sure you're doing them exactly right and doing them safely.

Warm-ups and Stretching at Home

When you practice your martial arts moves at home, you'll need to have your own warm-up and stretching routine. If you like, just repeat the same warm-ups and stretches you normally do in class. Or use the quick warm-up and stretch on the next few pages.

Start with something to get your heart beating faster; get yourself breathing hard and beginning to sweat. You might run laps around the yard, do jumping jacks, or march around the room lifting your knees high and pumping your fists high. If you're practicing with a friend and you have enough room, try a game of tag. Once you're sweating and breathing hard, go to the next step.

It's a good idea to move all the muscles and joints you'll be using when you practice your techniques, to make sure every part of you is warmed up. This is a little bit like checking out a race car before the race: You make sure the tires are in good condition and have enough air, the door opens and closes right, the seatbelt works properly, the engine is adjusted well, and there's enough gas in the tank.

When you're checking out your body before a workout, one way to remember what to do is to start at the top of your head and work your way down to your toes, making sure to move and use every part along the way.

Start at the top and work your way down.

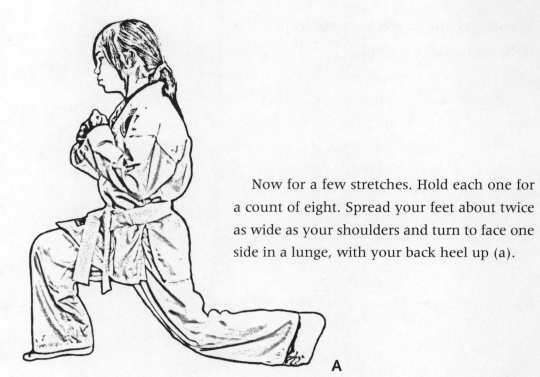

Now for a few stretches. Hold each one for a count of eight. Spread your feet about twice as wide as your shoulders and turn to face one side in a lunge, with your back heel up (a).

A

■ HINTS:

Keep your knee straight up above your foot; don't let your knee get ahead of your toes. Keep good posture while you're lunging. In fact, keep good posture all the time!

Now lunge to the other side. Then repeat the lunges, this time with your back heel down (b).

Next, drop down to one side with both feet flat (c).

Then do it again, but with your toes up (d). Don't forget to do each stretch to both sides.

B

C

D

Come back to the middle, so you're hanging down with your feet wide apart. Keep your knees a little bit bent and your back straight. Stay there for the count, then move to one side and count, then move to the other side.

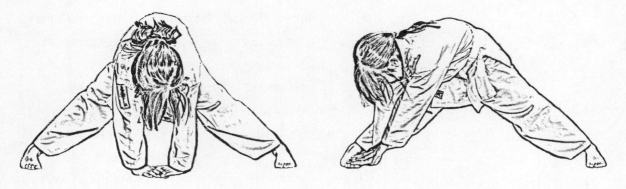

Move back to the middle again. Walk your hands forward and bring your feet together to stretch your calf muscles. The calf muscle is the muscle on the back of your lower leg. Once you're in position, push your heel gently down toward the floor. This will also stretch your Achilles tendon.

Next, walk your feet up to your hands and hang there. Let your knees be just a little bit bent. Can you put your hands flat on the floor without bending your knees a lot? If so, you're pretty flexible!

Now roll yourself up to standing. Pretend you're unrolling your backbone up toward the ceiling, until you're standing up straight.

One more stretch before we get to work on techniques: Bring one foot up behind your buttocks and grab it with your hand.

■ HINTS:

Keep your foot right behind you; don't twist it out to the side. Also, push your foot away from your buttocks instead of squeezing it in close.

This stretches your quadriceps, the muscle on the front of your thigh. Because you're standing on one foot, you can test your balance while you're stretching. If you start to wobble or lose your balance, go ahead and let go of your leg, so you can put your foot down and try again. Don't let yourself fall down! (If you need to, put your hand on a wall to keep your balance.) And remember to stretch both legs.

Now that you're warmed up and stretched, it's time to work on techniques.

Things to Do

1. Reasons to stretch.

At the beginning of this chapter, we learned two reasons for doing stretches. Do you remember what they are? (If you can't remember, look on page 42.)

The first reason to do stretches is _____.

When you're doing this kind of stretch, hold the stretch for a count of _____.

The second reason to do stretches is _____.

For this kind of stretch, hold it for at least _____.

2. Try this at home: opposite circles.

Remember when you did arm circles during warm-ups? You made big circles with one arm or both arms, going forward or backward. Try doing it with one arm moving forward and the other moving backward at the same time! Start with both hands up, then send one arm circling forward while the other arm circles backward.

Make sure they're really moving in opposite directions at the same time, not the same direction at different times.

3. Write down your warm-up routine.

Write down a list of warm-up and stretching exercises you can do from memory. Include exercises you do at your school, exercises from this book, and maybe even ones you learned doing another sport. Choose from this list when you do your warm-ups and stretches at home. You don't have to do all the exercises every time, but choose at least one exercise for every part of your body, starting with your head and working your way down.

_____

_____

_____

_____

_____

_____

"GOOD" STRETCHES AND "BAD" STRETCHES

Older martial artists will tell you that today's teachers know more about healthy stretching than their own teachers knew. Many of them grew up doing stretches that are now considered "bad."

One "bad" thing they used to do is bounce while stretching. If they were doing a lunge or reaching for their toes, for example, they'd take the proper position, then bounce up and down into the stretch. Today we know that bouncing causes many small injuries to the muscles and can actually make them *less* flexible instead of *more*.

Another example is the hurdler stretch, in which you sit on the floor with one leg stretched out in front and the other leg turned back behind you. We now know that this position is unhealthy for the knee that's turned behind—so we bring the leg in front instead. Any time you pull your heel in close to your buttocks, you squeeze your knee in a way that isn't good for it. If you sit or lie back on your heel while you do the stretch, that's even worse!

Many people did the "bad" exercises for years and turned out just fine. They were lucky. Other athletes weren't so lucky. They developed pain, injuries, and problems with their muscles and joints.

We can't tell in advance who is going to be lucky and who isn't. So the best bet is for everyone to stick with "good" stretches.

CHAPTER SEVEN

Practicing Your Art

From Chapter One until now, we have seen the word *practice* (or *practicing*) almost fifty times. Go back and count! And we're going to see it a lot more. That's because *practice* is one of the two most important words in the martial arts. (The other one is *respect*.)

You can't learn a martial art by reading or thinking about it, and you can't learn it by watching movies and videos. The only way to learn it is by doing it yourself. And it isn't enough to practice your moves a few times; you have to do them over and over.

A lot of your best practice will be in class. That's where you have your teacher to guide you, and your classmates to share the fun and hard work. Be sure to go to class at least two or three times a week.

Between classes, practice on your own. Follow your warm-up routine, then review what you've learned, work on improving your skills, and have fun while you do it!

This book is for when you practice at home. The next six chapters are about the *techniques* (stances, blocks, strikes, forms, and other exercises) you'll be learning in class. You'll find reminders of what you've learned and tips to help you know what to practice.

The techniques are organized into lessons, called levels, which build on each other. You may work your way through the lessons in order, but you don't have to. If the techniques you are practicing in class are found in different chapters, it's okay to skip around. Concentrate on what your teacher wants you to practice. Be sure to write down any differences between what your teacher says and what this book says about techniques, and pay close attention to your teacher.

For most techniques, you will see a name in English and, in parentheses, names in Japanese and Korean. Don't be surprised if your teacher has different names for some of the techniques. Even in one language, people don't always call things by the same name. For example, some people say *rising block,* where others say *high block,* and still others say *upper block.* They can all mean the same thing. So if the name given here is different from the one your teacher uses, make a note in the book. Use the name your teacher wants you to use.

Most of the techniques covered are things you'll need to master in order to earn higher belt ranks. They're the building blocks of your art. But keep these points in mind, too:

- There are other things besides *techniques* that are just as important, or maybe even more important, for earning belts—like etiquette, respect, good behavior, good attendance at the dojo, and strong effort.

- Your teacher is in charge of teaching you. This book is only for reminders and fun and maybe some extra help. Your teacher might want you to learn things in a different order. She or he might describe things in a different way, too. Always listen first to what your teacher has to say.

Things to Do
Rules for Practicing at Home

You need your parents' permission to practice at home. Then you and your parents need to agree on some rules. You must find out from your parents *where, when, what,* and *with whom* it's okay to practice. Now would be a great time to talk with your parents, and write down some of their answers here.

1. Where?

You'll need room to move safely without bumping into furniture, breakables, pets, or other people.

_____

_____

2. When?

There must always be an adult nearby. And there might be more limits, for example, "Only when your homework is done," or "Never after your little brother's bedtime."

_____

_____

3. What?

Always remember that martial arts moves are serious. They can hurt people. You must tell your parents what you want to practice, and they'll decide whether it's safe enough to practice at home. If you practice with a friend, avoid kicking or punching at each other, and never spar (pretend fight) outside the dojo or dojang. If there are other things your parents want you to avoid, write them down here:

_____

_____

_____

4. With whom?

It's fun to practice with a friend, but it should be a friend who also studies martial arts with a qualified teacher. You must not teach moves to your friends; that's their teachers' job. But you and your friends may practice what you have learned. Your parents need to know if someone wants to practice with you. They will decide whether it's okay for you to practice together.

_____

_____

_____

PART II

Training

Basics for a New
Martial Artist

During your first day or week of classes, you'll be shown many new things—stances, strikes, blocks, kicks, exercises. It's exciting to learn so much at once, and sometimes it's confusing. Don't worry if you feel confused, because the things you learn at the very beginning are things you'll be practicing again and again, during every class. You'll have plenty of time to learn them and make them better. And most likely, this will be the only time you have to learn so many new things at once. Later on your teachers will add new skills a few at a time, when they can see you're ready.

Stances

Martial arts has many stances, or ways of standing, depending on what we're doing or what we want to do next. Here are some important ones:

Ready Stance, or Natural Stance
(hachiji dachi, junbi sogi)

This is how to stand when you line up for class, when you're listening to the teacher, or when you're waiting to find out what comes next. When you're practicing, you'll begin and end many exercises in this stance. Your feet should be as wide as your shoulders.

Attention Stance
(musubi dachi, charyŏt sogi)

You'll use this stance every time you get ready to bow—like at the beginning of class when the instructor calls out *Attention, bow!* When you hear *attention*—pull your hands and feet in! Your heels should be touching. In some styles, the feet are straight with the toes together. Which way do you do it at your school? Put a star next to the correct feet.

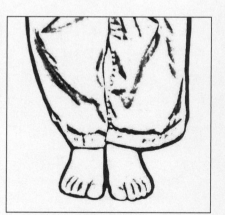

Rectangular Stance *(shiko dachi)* and Straddle-leg or Horse Stance *(kiba dachi, juchŭm sogi)*

In almost every class, students practice punches in rectangular stance or horse stance. If you're doing it right, your legs will get really tired, but the practice will improve your strength and endurance. For rectangular stance, the feet are angled slightly outward, as they were in natural stance. It's different in straddle-leg or horse stance: the feet are both straight. Which way do you practice at your school? Put a star next to the right picture.

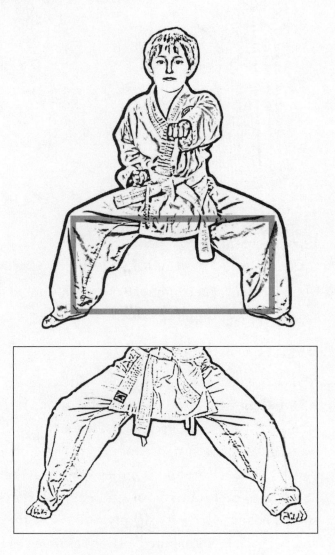

■ TIPS:

Do you see any reason to call it *rectangular* stance? If the shape your legs make is more like a *triangle* than a *rectangle*, you're up too high! Bend your knees more to get lower.

Forward Stance
(zenkutsu dachi, ap-gubi sogi)

You'll do a lot of techniques in forward stance, so work hard to do excellent forward stances when you're practicing.

■ TIPS:

Make sure your stance is long enough: take a big step. Make sure it's wide enough: don't walk on a tightrope. It should be more like walking on a railroad track with one foot on each rail. When you're standing in forward stance, notice that you have a front leg and a back leg. Make sure the front leg is bent so that the knee is right above your foot (but not forward over your toes). Your front foot should be turned in very slightly. Make sure the back leg is straight and the back foot is pointed forward as much as you can. Your heel should be flat on the floor—don't let it come up. Push your hips forward and keep good posture. The arrow in the picture indicates good posture.

Forward Parallel Stance or Walking Stance
(moro ashi dachi, ap sogi)

This stance is almost as easy as just standing and walking. It's easy to move quickly in this stance. With just a small change of turning your body away slightly, it makes a good *fighting stance* (see below).

Fighting Stance
(kumite dachi, kyorugi sogi)

This is one kind of fighting stance, but there are many possibilities. Your teacher will show you.

Knee Up, or Kicking Stance

This one is good for practicing your balance and strengthening the muscles that lift your knee. You can do all your kicks from here, too, because they all start with lifting your knee. That's why we call it *kicking stance* in Cuong Nhu, but not everyone calls it that.

■ TIPS:

Don't let your knee sag! Keep it up high, so you could balance a bowl of soup on it if you wanted to. Holding your knee up is what makes you stronger.

Serpent Stance

Also called *drop stance* or *snake stance*, this is used in warm-ups to stretch the legs. But advanced students use it in sparring to drop down low and do spinning footsweeps. Why do you think it's called serpent stance?

_____

_____

Hand Techniques

How to Make a Tight Fist

If you want to learn to punch, you'll need a tight fist. That will keep you from hurting your fingers and thumb when you hit a target or punching bag.

Start with your hand open and your fingers tight together. Roll your fingers down, keeping them tight together, until your fist is completely closed and you can't see your fingernails. Then lock your thumb across the front of your fingers.

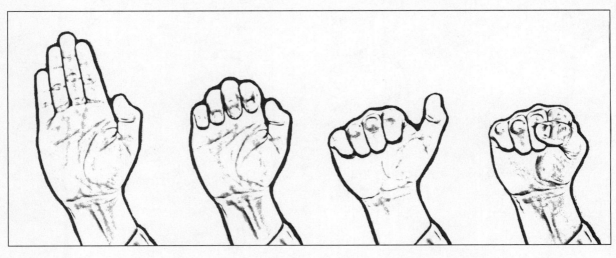

■ TIPS:

Don't put your thumb inside! Make sure your wrist is straight, and hold it straight when you punch.

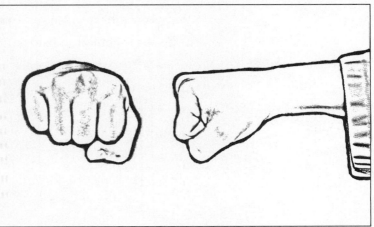

Horizontal Punch
(choku-zuki, ap chirŭgi)

This is probably the punch you'll practice most. When teachers just say *punch*, this is usually what they mean. Start with your fist on your side (up against your ribs), palm side up. To punch with that fist, shoot it out toward an imaginary (or real) target in front of you; and at the very last second, twist your fist so it ends palm side down.

■ TIPS:

Keep your elbow close to your side when the punch is going out. At the same time one fist is on its way out to punch, pull the other one back to your side so it will be ready for the next punch. (See "Action and Reaction" on page 71 for more about this.)

Protect your elbow: don't straighten it all the way at the end of the punch!

Three Punches, Three Levels:
High *(jodan, sang dan)*, **Middle** *(chudan, jung dan)*,
and Low *(gedan, arae)*

Practice them one at a time or try putting all three together as quickly as you can do them: high-middle-low (left-right-left), then low-middle-high (right-left-right).

■ TIPS:

The high punch should be aimed at face level—your own face level—not over your head! Only punch as fast as you can punch without getting sloppy or taking shortcuts (like not pulling your other hand all the way back each time).

In class, when you're punching in rectangular or horse stance, you might do a hundred punches or more at each level—trying to hold a strong, low rectangular stance the whole time. It's really hard! Your legs get very tired. Practicing this way helps build strength, stamina, and determination. Always try your best, even if it's hard and you're getting tired. And even if you're tired, keep good posture. Don't let yourself slouch or lean over. Posture is very important!

Shifting Punches

This is another way to build strength and stamina while practicing punches. Start in rectangular stance, then bend the left knee and straighten the right leg, so you're lunging to your left. Punch back the opposite way with the right fist. On the next count shift over to the opposite side and punch back toward the left.

■ TIPS:

Turn and look first, then shift and punch. It's always a good idea to see where (or what or whom) you're punching. Try not to lean your body way over to the side. Use your legs to make you lean to one side or the other, but keep your body upright.

It helps to imagine attackers when you practice these. Picture your attackers right in front of you, throwing attacks right at the center of your body or at your head. You protect yourself by lunging out of the way (shifting to one side) so they miss you, and punching back toward them.

Lunge Punch *(oi-zuki, baro chirŭgi)* **and**
Reverse Punch *(gyaku-zuki, bandae chirŭgi)*

Remember how, in forward stance, you have a front leg and a back
leg? If you're punching with the arm that goes with the front leg,
it's called *lunge punch*. If you're punching with the arm that goes
with the back leg, it's called *reverse punch*. So if you're in left forward
stance, punching with your left fist, it's lunge punch. But if you're
in left forward stance and punch with your right fist, it's reverse
punch. What if you're in *right* forward stance, punching with your
left fist? What's that punch called? _____

Inner Chop *(uchi shuto-uchi, son-nal backat chigi)*

Start with your palm to your opposite-side ear, and your other hand extended in front. Turn your hand palm down as you chop, pulling the other hand back to your side at the same time, just as you did when you were punching.

■ TIPS:

Sometimes we use another name for the *starting position* of a technique. We call it the *load* position or *chamber* position. Always *load* before you *strike*, just as you would load a weapon (or put a bullet in the *chamber*) before firing at a target.

A Good Chopping Hand or Knifehand

Be sure your hand is tight, your fingers are tight together, and your thumb is pulled up tight along the side of your hand. Your hand shouldn't be cupped at all. If it is, it will collapse when it hits the target, and you could injure your hand. No thumbs or fingers sticking up—they could also get injured. Strike the target with the side of your hand—the "knife-edge"—not your fingers or your arm.

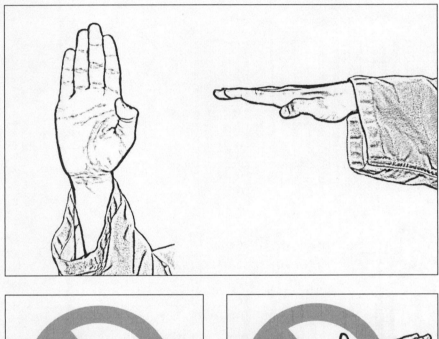

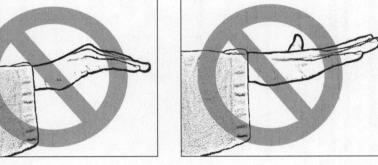

Shifting Inner Chop

A great exercise—a lot like shifting punches.

Lower Block
(gedan-barai, arae-makgi)

The starting position, or load position, is a lot like inner chop, but with fists. To block, swing the fist down from your ear to catch your attacker's arm or leg on the side and knock it out of the way. Don't forget to pull your other fist back to the ready-to-punch position.

■ TIP:

Remember, load before you block. That's a big part of what makes your block strong.

Rising Block *(jodan-age-uke, sang dan makgi)*

Start with your arms across in front of you, one stacked above the other. The arm on top is palm facing down; the lower arm is palm facing up. The lower arm will do the block, and the other arm will pull back to your ribs, ready to punch. Make sure the blocking arm passes in front of your face on the way up! Otherwise, someone could punch you in the nose, and your block wouldn't help.

■ TIPS:

Think of putting a "roof" over your head to protect your head. A rising block is like a roof that slants from one side to the other. Make sure your whole head is under the roof. And make sure there's some space in the "attic"—don't have the roof resting on your head! Actually, this kind of roof isn't really *above* your head; your arm should be out in front, where you can see it just by raising your eyes. A flat roof isn't so good. If something heavy falls on it, it might crash down on top of your head. Make the roof slanted, so heavy things can roll off the side. Can you circle what's wrong in the two pictures?

Blocking a Punch

As a punch comes toward your nose, catch it from underneath and deflect it upward away from your head.

Leg Techniques

Upward Knee Kick
(*mae hiza geri, murŭp ollyo chagi*)

The knee swings upward (or forward) to strike your attacker in the groin. For the strongest kick, start in forward stance and use the back leg to kick. When you're practicing in the air—without a partner—swing up high and strong to exercise your leg muscles and challenge your balance. Strong muscles and good balance are important to good martial artists.

ACTION AND REACTION

Sir Isaac Newton once said, "For every action, there is an equal and opposite reaction." He wasn't talking about karate techniques, but martial arts teachers like to borrow his words to describe how to do a good, strong strike or block.

A good, strong hand technique—a punch, chop, or block—doesn't use just one hand or arm; it uses both arms.

Think about practicing a punch. One fist starts on your side, and you throw it forward to punch. At the same time, the other arm pulls back, all the way till your other fist is on your side and your elbow is back behind you. (Now *that* fist is ready to punch.)

The hand doing the punch is the *action hand.* The one pulling back to your side at the same time is the *reaction hand.* Both the action hand and the reaction hand need to be fast and strong. In fact, they should be equally fast and strong, going in opposite directions.

Remember how to do an inner chop? From the starting position (one palm near your ear, the other one thrust out in front of you), you chop out from your ear toward the target, while at the same time pulling the other hand back to your side.

The hand doing the chop is the action hand, and the hand pulling back to your side is the reaction hand. The two of them should be equally strong.

What you *don't* want to do is try to do a strong punch, chop, or block with one arm, while the other arm just hangs around taking a rest. All good strikes and blocks use both arms equally. Every action hand has an equal and opposite reaction hand!

For more on the why and how of action and reaction, see Appendix B: The Physics of Action and Reaction, on page 171.

Front Snap Kick
(mae-geri-keage, ap chagi)

Start by raising your knee, just like upward knee kick. Then swing your foot out to strike with the ball of your foot. Pull your toes up! If you don't . . . ouch! Your toes will jam into the target.

■ TIP:

Remember to pull your foot back before you step down. Don't let your foot and leg just fall to the floor after you kick.

Escaping Techniques

Escaping techniques are things you do to get away from someone who is attacking or grabbing you. You'll need a partner to practice these techniques. Remember to bow to your partner and practice *respectfully* and *carefully*. Follow your teacher's instructions *exactly*. Avoid doing anything that might hurt your partner. For example, when you're practicing a choke technique, don't really choke your partner! Do a "pretend" choke, without touching your partner's throat (but you may touch their shoulders).

Ducking Out of a Choke

If someone is trying to grab or choke you, the best thing is to get loose as fast as you can and get away, without getting into a fight. This technique is a good example: you just tuck your chin, duck your head under one of your attacker's arms, twist out, and run away.

■ TIP:

Any time someone is reaching to try to grab your neck—even if it's in class for practice—always tuck your chin down to protect your throat. This makes it harder for someone to choke you. You might need that extra advantage to help you get away.

Things to Do

Answers are on page 78.

1. Name the techniques.

What are these students doing? Write the names of the techniques under the pictures.

_____   _____

2. What's wrong with this picture?

This student is trying hard, but he could do better. He's practicing a punch (what kind?—write the name under the picture) in a certain stance (which stance?), but something else isn't as good as it should be. Can you circle what it is? Then he fixes the first mistake, but makes a different mistake in the second picture. Circle that one, too. If you need a hint, re-read the tips on page 58–59.

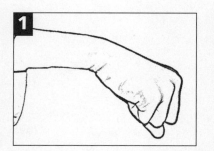

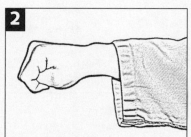

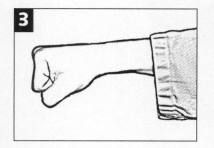

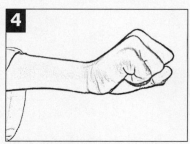

3. Which fist would you punch with?

Here are four fists, but three of them are making big mistakes! Can you see what's wrong? Draw a circle with a line through it over the three bad ones, and put a star next to the one *you* would use. If you need help, reread page 61.

4. Basic training: make your own workout.

There are lots of ways to practice at home. Here's one way: After warm-ups, start with thirty punches in rectangular or horse stance. Then see if you can remember all your basic techniques. First do all your hand techniques (punches, chops) ten times each. Then do all your blocks ten times each. Then do your kicks ten times each. Now choose three special techniques for extra work, including one hand technique, one block, and one kick. Do these thirty times each moving in forward stance, trying to make each one better than the last. At the end if you're tired, sweaty, and out of breath—you've done a good job! If you aren't—do it all again!

5. Try this at home: bowing.

What if you had to bow upon entering and leaving your room at home? It isn't such a crazy idea; after all, your room is a special place. You spend a lot of time there, and it reflects what kind of person you are. Try it for a week. Bow when you go in to remind yourself that your room is special. Then look around. Have you been treating it as though it's special? If something is messy, tidy it up. If things are out of place, put them away. If you share your room with a brother or sister, set a good example for sharing and keeping things neat.

Is there something you can do to make your room more special— like hang a picture or arrange the furniture in a new way (with your parents' permission, of course)? Try to make your room the very best it can be.

Enjoy your time in your room and make the most of it. For example, if you do homework in your room, do it right away and do your very best. If you have friends over to play, have a great time, then work together to put away your books and toys.

ANSWERS:

Name the techniques. The student on the left is doing *reverse punch.* The student on the right is doing *front snap kick.* **What's wrong with this picture?** He's doing *lunge punch* in *forward stance.* But he has *very bad posture*—he's leaning forward! In the next picture his posture is better, but now his *back heel is up.* He should fix that. **Which fist would you punch with?** Not 1 or 4—they both have bent wrists. Not 2—it has its thumb on the inside! All three mistakes can cause injury. Use number 3: tight fist, straight wrist.

Introduction to Self-Defense

In Level Two we learn some new techniques, and we spend a lot of time talking about self-defense. Self-defense is all about protecting yourself and staying safe. Besides fun and exercise, there are many important reasons for learning a martial art, and self-defense is one of them. For some people, it's the number one reason. They want to learn blocks, kicks, punches, and other fighting techniques, so they can learn how to protect themselves in a fight. Fighting techniques are good things to know, but there's a lot more to self-defense than fighting.

The Five A's of Self-Defense

Good martial artists know the most important part of self-defense is what happens *before* a fight begins, *before* you find yourself in trouble. The most important tools of self-defense aren't *physical* techniques—like blocks, kicks, and punches—but *mental* techniques that use common sense and good judgment. These are the tools that keep you from doing dangerous things, help you see trouble coming before it happens, and help you get out of bad spots before things get worse.

Every good martial artist knows these two things:

- *The best way to win a fight is not to get in it in the first place.*

- *The best way to get out of trouble is to avoid getting in it in the first place.*

Martial artists never want to fight, because they know how serious fighting is. They know they could hurt someone, they could get hurt, and everyone could get in a lot of trouble. They know that even though others might use violence, they—as martial artists— have special skills and special responsibilities. They'll do everything they can to avoid conflict, and if they can't avoid it, they'll try anything to resolve it peacefully, without fighting.

And self-defense isn't just about fights, it's about staying out of all kinds of trouble. O'Sensei Ngo Dong, the founder of Cuong Nhu karate, taught the Five A's of Self-Defense to help students protect themselves and stay out of trouble:

Awareness   **Alertness**

Avoidance   **Anticipation**

Action

Read more about the Five A's in the next few pages. Talk to your parents about them.

Now let's look at a few new techniques. Pay attention to which of these we use later, in the section about escaping techniques.

Hand Techniques

Remember the inner chop you learned in Level One? A longer name for inner chop is inner horizontal chop. *Horizontal* means "flat" or "side to side" (along the horizon). An inner horizontal chop starts on the inside and moves along the horizon toward the outside.

Vertical Chop *(otoshi shuto uchi, son-nal sewo chigi)*

Vertical is the opposite of *horizontal;* it means "up and down." For a vertical chop, start *up* and strike *down*.

Remember, keep a tight hand and tight fingers, and strike with the knife-edge!

Inner Middle Block *(uchi ude-uke, backat jung dan makgi)*

Start with your arms across in front of you with one below the other, both palms facing down, and tight fists. Remember, the arm on the bottom is the one that will do the block. Swing it up and to the side, snapping into place with the palm of your fist facing your shoulder. Pull the other arm back, ready to punch.

THE FIVE A'S OF SELF-DEFENSE: AWARENESS

Awareness is *knowledge*. Are you *aware* that fire is dangerous? That it's unsafe to play in the street? That you shouldn't talk to strangers or go with them? Do you *know* some kids who get in fights and trouble all the time? Are you *aware* of some places where you shouldn't go alone, and others where you shouldn't go at all? Did you *know* you might avoid a fight just by using good manners?

You didn't always know these things; you had to learn them. Maybe you have a younger sister or brother who doesn't know, and you can help them learn. Your parents know a lot, and they want to help you learn.

TALK TO YOUR PARENTS

What do you need to be *aware* of in order to keep yourself safe?

■ TIPS:

To begin the block, don't hold your arms up too high (above your shoulders). They should be low and near your body. When you finish the block, your fist should be about even with your shoulder, not way up high or sagging down low. Don't scrunch your arm up too tight and close to your body. And remember to keep your wrist straight!

Blocking a Punch

As the punch comes toward you, catch it on the *inside* and move it to the *outside*, just far enough so that it misses you. Strike with the *side* of your arm, not the *back* of your arm.

Another Way to Do Middle Block

Some schools and styles finish the middle block by snapping the wrist so the palm faces outward (instead of facing back toward the shoulder). And remember what we said about people calling things by different names? What we called *inner* middle block because it *starts* on the *inside,* some schools call *outside* block because it *moves* toward the *outside.* Often, the Japanese and Korean names will have this difference between them.

Leg Techniques

Roundhouse Knee Kick
(mawashi hiza geri, murŭp tol ryŏ chagi)

This is a really difficult kick, and it's very important for self-defense. It might look simple, but to do it just right and with power takes a lot of practice. Many students find it harder to do than the roundhouse kick and other more advanced kicks. When do you think you would use a roundhouse knee kick instead of an upward knee kick?

■ TIPS:

Don't let your foot hang down. Make your whole leg *horizontal* if you can—just as it is in the picture. The foot you're standing on needs to turn out, or *pivot,* so your hip can turn properly for a powerful kick. If you don't let your foot pivot, you could hurt your knee (the knee of the leg you're standing on). If you have trouble pivoting your foot, then turn it—toes out—before you kick.

Escaping Techniques

One thing we learn for self-defense is how to *escape from grabs,* or how to get loose when someone tries to grab hold of you. In order to get good at these escaping techniques, we have to practice them in class with our classmates grabbing us. So we all need to learn how to do certain grabs together, to help each other practice.

The Nine Grabs

See if you can match these nine names to the nine pictures. Write the names under the pictures.

1. Same-side wrist grab

2. Opposite-side or cross-hand wrist grab

3. Both wrists (two hands on two)

4. Two hands on one

5. Both wrists from behind

6. One shoulder

7. Both shoulders

8. Choke

9. Bear hug from behind

There are other ways of grabbing, too, but these are the ones we'll start with.

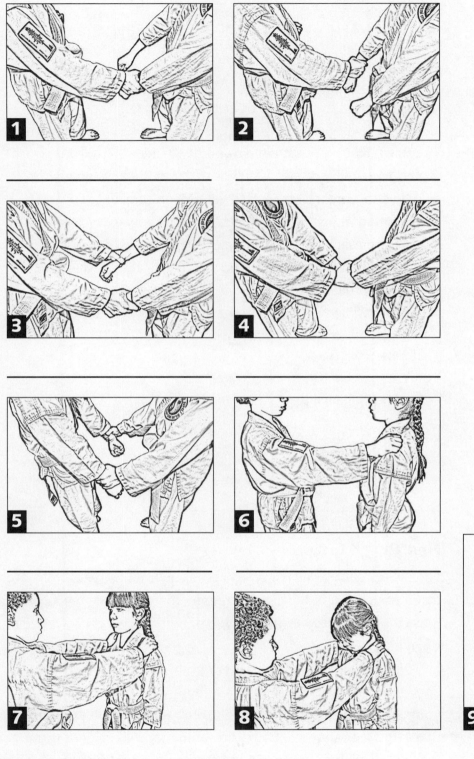

THE FIVE A'S OF SELF-DEFENSE: ALERTNESS

Alertness is paying attention and noticing things. It means watching out. You have to be *alert* when you're riding your bike, so you don't bump into anyone. You have to be *alert* when you're crossing the street, so you don't step out in front of a car. You should be *alert* any time you're outside, so you notice who else is around you. Is that your friend coming toward you, or is it a stranger or the school bully? Is someone in your group of friends angry and ready to pick a fight?

If you don't notice things, you won't be ready to protect yourself if you need to. Some habits can make you less *alert*—like reading while walking or talking on a cell phone. Even listening to music on headphones makes you less *alert*. A good martial artist will always stay *alert*.

TALK TO YOUR PARENTS

Are there times when it's especially important to be *alert?* Are there things you sometimes do that make it harder for you to be *alert?*

First Thumb Escape

The first thumb escape is a way to get loose from grab #1. There are many ways to get out of a grab. Thumb escape is a good one because it teaches an important rule of self-defense: *Find your attacker's weak spot and take advantage of it.*

What's the weak spot on a wrist grab? Try this: Use your right hand to grab your left arm. Look at how your hand closes around your arm. If there's a little gap between your thumb and fingers, that's the weak spot; your left arm should try to break out through the gap. But if the hand is big and strong enough, there won't be a gap. Then where's the weak spot? Write your answer here. (Hint: look for the smallest, thinnest part of the grab.)

Thumb escapes are good because even if the person grabbing your wrist is bigger and stronger than you are, chances are your arm is bigger and stronger than their thumb. Your arm plus your whole body is definitely bigger and stronger than their thumb. You can use the force of your whole body to break out of their grasp by breaking out against their thumb. It has a good chance of working, *if:*

- You do it correctly.

- You do it at the right time.

- You do it suddenly and without warning.

- You do it with power and confidence, and give it everything you've got.

Even then it might not work, because nothing is guaranteed. A good martial artist will be ready to try something else if the first technique doesn't work. And they'll keep trying until they succeed, or at least until they've done the very best they can do.

Counterattacks and Follow-up Techniques

When you look at the pictures for the first thumb escape, you'll see a student escaping from grab #1, then fighting back with chops, punches, and knee kicks. Remember when you learned the *ducking out* choke escape? We learned then that the best thing is to escape and run away without getting in a fight. That's still true! If you can do thumb escape and run away, that's what you should do.

As martial artists, we also have to practice for those serious times when we can't just run away—when we have to hit back hard enough that our attacker can't come after us again. So we learn *counterattacks* (striking back) and *follow-up techniques* (more strikes, throws, or pins to make sure we did enough to stop our attacker).

We practice them hard, so if we ever have to use them, we'll have a better chance of succeeding. That's why we practice striking back after the thumb escapes.

But how do you know when to run away, when to hit back, and when to try just talking? That's the hard part. Find out what your parents and your teachers think when you're talking to them about the Five A's of Self-Defense.

Tips on the First Thumb Escape:

Don't forget to step *forward and slightly to the side* at the same time you break your wrist free. Get behind the attacker's back if you can. If your attacker grabs your right wrist with grab #1, step forward and to the right with your right foot. (What should you do if they grab your left wrist?)

THE FIVE A'S OF SELF-DEFENSE: AVOIDANCE

Avoidance means staying away from people, places, and things that can get you hurt or get you in trouble. If you're *aware* and you're *alert,* then most of the time you'll be able to *avoid.* For example, if there's a busy street with lots of traffic, don't go there; ride your bike somewhere else! If the school bully is hanging around the swing set, go play somewhere else! If a stranger is walking toward you, walk quickly the other way or over to your parents. If your classmate is angry and wants to fight, try being nice to them, but if that doesn't help, walk away. If there's an adult—even if they aren't a stranger—who makes you feel bad or uncomfortable, *avoid* them if you can and especially *avoid* being alone with them.

TALK TO YOUR PARENTS:

What people, places, and things do they think you should *avoid?* What people, places, and things do *you* think you should *avoid?* Why? What should you do if you can't avoid them completely—for example, if they're in your class or in your family? What if there's a dangerous place you have to pass by on your way to school?

■ MORE TIPS:

The motion of breaking free is like getting ready to do an inner chop: Snap your hand up to your opposite-side ear. Use your free hand to stick to, or *jam,* your attacker's arm while you chop, then immediately follow up with punches and a knee kick. Which knee should you use? (The one that's still in front of the attacker!)

What kind of knee kick do you think would work best?

Moving to the Dead Side

When you escape, be careful not to step to the side where your attacker has a free hand waiting to punch you or a leg waiting to kick you. We call that the *live* side, because it has "live ammunition." Go to the *dead* side, where they have fewer ways to hit you. Usually "moving to the dead side" means moving behind the arm or leg that was attacking you, or trying to get behind your attacker's back. Here's what moving to the dead side looks like when the attacker punches.

 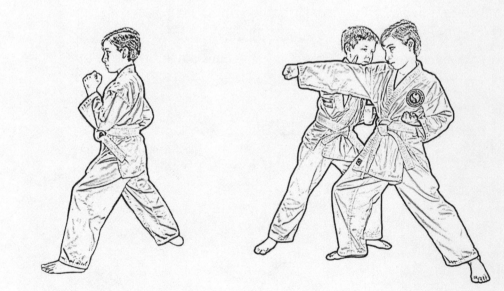

THE FIVE A'S OF SELF-DEFENSE: ANTICIPATION

Anticipation means thinking ahead, not waiting until trouble comes to you. For example, if some scary-looking kids are walking toward you and you think they might be planning to hit you, you don't have to wait till they get there to find out! Take off quickly toward the nearest responsible grown-up (parent or teacher). And just in case, get ready to duck, block, and escape. If it turns out they weren't going to bother you—no harm done!

Anticipating and planning ahead are important for keeping yourself safe. Does your family have an emergency plan in case of fire, earthquake, or storm? Do you know what it is? Do you know how and when to call for help by dialing 911?

TALK TO YOUR PARENTS

What would they like you to do in an emergency? What do they think you should do if someone tries to get you to fight? Are there things you worry about that you can plan ahead for? For example, some kids worry about what to do if there's a robber in the house, or if a bigger kid tries to steal their backpack. Talk about what you could do and act out different ideas. Sometimes *anticipating* trouble makes it less scary, in case it ever really happens.

Windmill Escape from Choke

Remember, if you think someone might try to choke you, immediately put your chin down to make it harder for them to grab your throat. Always practice this way, even though you know your partner won't really choke you. Now raise one arm, like the blade of a windmill, and twist back away from your attacker as your arm passes over their arms. Use your whole body. As you spin free, your "windmill" hand goes to your ear, ready for an inner chop. Turn back toward your attacker, then chop, punch, and knee kick.

■ TIPS:

Windmill doesn't work by hitting or pushing your attacker's arms. If your attacker is bigger and stronger than you, all your hitting and pushing might not work. Instead, spin your windmill blade right over the top of his or her arms as if they weren't even there.

THE FIVE A'S OF SELF-DEFENSE:
ACTION

Action means *doing something!* All the other A's involve doing
something: learning things, watching out, staying away from
dangers, and planning ahead (that is, having a plan of *action*).
And finally, if something bad does happen, you should be ready
to do whatever it takes to protect yourself and get safe. If something bad happens, you might be really scared, but you won't
freeze up. You'll do something; and if that doesn't work, you'll
try something else; and you won't stop trying until you're safe.
That's the kind of courage and determination a martial artist
practices every day.

Sometimes the best *action* is just running away! Sometimes
it's calling 911. Sometimes it's using friendly words; other times,
you might need to shout for help. If a bully is trying to punch
you in the nose, you might need to duck, block, use words—
and run!

In a serious emergency, if nothing else works, you might
need to use kicks and punches—but that's the very last thing
you should ever want to do. Still, in a serious emergency—like
a stranger trying to take you to a car—you must do everything
you can to get away.

TALK TO YOUR PARENTS

What do they think is the best *action* to take if trouble happens? When is running away best, and when is it better to use
words? What is and what isn't a serious emergency? Do your
parents think it's ever okay to use kicks and punches? Do you
think so? When is it okay?

Things to Do

Answers are on page 96.

1. Name the techniques.

The Japanese names for the nine grabs are in the box below. Go back to page 85 and write them under the corresponding pictures. If you use Korean words or different names for the grabs at your school, write those here and under the pictures.

Same-side grab:	*Katate dori*
Opposite-side grab:	*Gyakute dori*
Two hands on two:	*Ryote dori*
Two hands on one:	*Morote dori*
Two hands from behind:	*Ushiro ryote dori*
One shoulder:	*Kata dori*
Both shoulders:	*Ryo kata dori*
Choke:	*Jime*
Bear hug from behind:	*Ushiro dori*

2. What's wrong with this picture?

This student is practicing a kick. One of the pictures shows him doing a good job. In the other, he's making at least two mistakes. Write the name of the technique under the good picture and circle the mistakes in the other picture. See page 83 if you need some hints.

3. Which one is the best chopping hand?

Put a star next to the hand that's ready to do a good chop. Draw a circle with a line through it over the ones that are making mistakes. If you need help, look back at page 67.

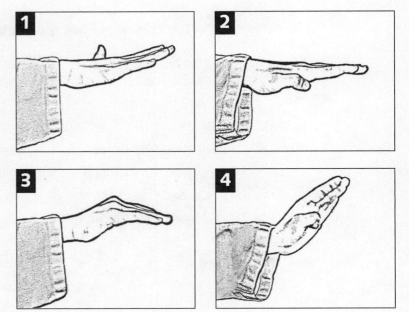

4. Basic training: knee kicks over obstacles.

An "obstacle" is something that's in the way. For example, if you try to practice roundhouse knee kick when you're standing too close to a bookcase, your knee is going to bang into the bookcase (ouch!). But if a low chair or coffee table is in the way, or maybe your bed, you should be able to do your roundhouse knee kick over the obstacle and bring it all the way back without bumping into anything. If your knee goes over but your ankle bangs into it, you aren't holding your leg correctly, and you need more practice! Try it: Find an obstacle that is higher than your knee. (Your bed might work, and because your mattress is soft, it's a safe choice. Whatever you choose, get your parents' permission first!) Start in forward stance facing the obstacle, do a roundhouse knee kick over it, then bring your leg back to forward stance without touching. Be sure you're close enough to really reach over the obstacle with your knee!

Remember "Make Your Own Workout" from Level One (see page 77)? This could be one of your special three techniques for your workout.

5. Try this at home: meditation.

Remember how you meditated at the beginning and end of class? You might have been kneeling with your hands on your knees or sitting cross-legged. Or maybe you were standing up straight and relaxed, with your heels touching and your fingertips touching lightly in front of you. You were breathing easily—in and out—and letting all your thoughts, feelings, and distractions float away so you could focus your mind on practicing.

Meditation can help outside the dojo. For example, sometimes you might get angry or lose your temper. (It happens to everyone now and then.) Next time something makes you mad and you're about to lose your temper, instead of saying or doing something you'll regret, stop yourself and try meditating. Assume meditation stance and breathe in and out at least ten times. Notice your angry feelings, then let them float away. When you open your eyes, see if you can solve the problem with calm words.

If there's something you're supposed to do, but you feel too tired and don't want to do it, try meditating for a few moments. As you breathe in and out, imagine you're breathing energy and excitement into your body. When you open your eyes, be ready to do your very best at whatever you have to do.

ANSWERS:

What's wrong with this picture? The student is practicing a roundhouse knee kick. In the second picture, he isn't letting his supporting foot turn to allow him to finish a strong kick. He's also letting his kicking leg sag. If he kicked over an obstacle, he'd bang his ankle! **Which one is the best chopping hand?** Not 1 or 3: one has a thumb sticking up; the other is "cupped" and will collapse if it hits something. Not 4: it has a bent wrist, and the thumb isn't in the right place. Use number 2: straight and tight.

LEVEL THREE

Ready in Every Direction

In Level Three we're going to pay close attention to something you've probably already done a lot in class: turning. When you're practicing moves across the floor and you get to the end, you turn. When you're practicing self-defense with partners, you might have to turn to face them or turn to move away. When you learn forms or patterns (more about this later), you have to turn in many directions, using several different ways of turning.

Why do you think it's important to practice turning?

_____

_____

_____

A good martial artist is ready for anything. One part of that is being *aware* and *alert,* knowing what's going on all around you. The next part is being ready to turn in any direction—to greet your friends, face your attackers, or avoid something dangerous. You should be ready to turn using either your left foot or your right foot. You should be able to turn quickly and easily without thinking. You should be able to turn around fast into a good stance without losing your balance, so you can block, kick, or strike, if necessary. Turning is an important skill for self-defense.

Turning in Forward Stance

You've probably heard your instructor give the command *turn!* *(mawatte, dorra)*. We're going to look at four different ways of turning, each one with its own name. There are other ways to turn, too; but if you can master these four, you won't have trouble doing *any* kind of turn. Most of the time when you hear the command to turn, you'll do the first one—the one we call *reverse*. If your instructor uses different names for this turn or the others, write those names above or below the pictures.

When you're learning these turns, it's helpful to imagine a compass on the floor, showing north, south, east, and west. Know which direction you're facing when you begin each turn, and see where you end up.

Reverse

This one is tricky. You only get to move your back foot. Leave your front foot where it is, almost as if it were stuck to the floor, but let it *pivot* (turn in place). When you're done, the back foot (the one that moved) has become your front foot. So if you start in left for-

ward stance, facing north, and do *reverse*, you should end in *right* forward stance, facing south.

■ TIPS:

If the wrong foot is in front when you finish, maybe you moved your back foot around too far. Or maybe you accidentally let your front foot take a step after you turned.

90-Degree Turn

This is a turn to one side—either the right or the left—using your front foot. If your right foot is in front, you'll turn to the right. If your left foot is in front, you'll turn to the left. Your back foot stays in place but *pivots*. If you start in left forward stance, facing west, you'll end in left forward stance, facing south.

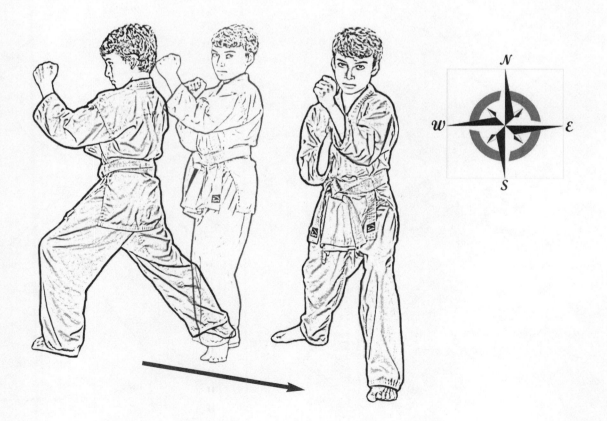

180-Degree Turn

Your front foot moves on this turn. Start in forward stance. Draw your front foot all the way back to your other foot then past the *heel* of your other foot, continuing on until you're facing the opposite direction in forward stance. If you start in left forward stance, facing east, you'll end in left forward stance, facing west.

■ TIP:

Remember, one foot passes behind the *heel* (not toes) of the other foot.

270-Degree Turn

This is like a *reverse* that went too far. As in reverse, your back foot moves and ends up becoming your front foot. So if you start in right forward stance, you end in left forward stance. Also like reverse, your front foot stays stuck to the floor but *pivots*. But with reverse, if you start facing north, you end up facing south. With 270-degree turn, if you start facing north, your back foot moves so far around behind you that you pass the south and end up facing *east!*

■ TIP:

Any time you need to pivot your foot—when turning and on many of your kicks—be careful to let your foot turn easily. If you leave it behind and don't pivot correctly, you'll twist your knee and your hip. You could injure yourself.

Hand Techniques

Double Rising Block
(morote jodan uke, du sang dan makgi)

Do you remember how to do a rising block? For double rising block, use both arms at once. Start with your wrists crossed, palm side up; then your block opens up and out. If rising block is like a slanted roof over your head, double rising block is like a roof that comes to a point above your head and slants both ways.

■ TIPS:

Many of the tips for rising block apply here, too. Keep some space in the "attic"! Block up and forward, away from your head—not back on top of your head. Keep your wrists straight!

Double Vertical Chop
(morote otoshi-shuto-uchi, du son-nal sewo chigi)

This one also uses both arms at once. Try putting double rising block and double vertical chop together in a combination.

Leg Techniques

Roundhouse Kick
(mawashi geri, tol ryǒ chagi)

If you have been practicing your roundhouse knee kick, round-house kick will be easy. Start with a roundhouse knee kick, then let your lower leg swing out and strike the target with the ball of your foot.

Sometimes we strike with the top of the foot, or *instep,* instead. For that kind of roundhouse kick, point your foot and point your toes.

Escaping Techniques

Second Thumb Escape

Let's try thumb escape against a different grab. This time your attacker will grab your wrist with grab #2. Which grab is that?

_____ (Hint: See page 85.)

Now use the same ideas we used before against grab #1: Step forward and to the side while using your arm to break out against the attacker's thumb. Don't step toward your attacker's free hand, because it might punch you! Step to the other side. What's that side called?

_____ (Hint: See page 90.)

Use your free hand to jam their arm while you follow up with a punch, then a knee kick—using the knee that's still in front of the attacker (that means, use your back leg).

In the first thumb escape, the motion of breaking free was like getting ready to do what technique?

_____ (Hint: See page 90.)

For the second thumb escape, the attacker's thumb is on the other side, so you can't just do the same thing as before. This time the motion is like doing an inner middle block.

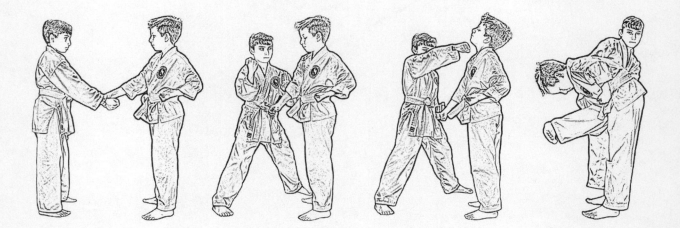

■ TIPS:

Break free using the quickest and easiest way out. Instead of going against your attacker's hand or getting tangled up with their arm, find the way to pop your arm right out past their thumb. Don't try to just pull your arm free. They'll pull back, and you'll have a tug-of-war with your arm. Instead, snap it out with a twisting motion of your wrist. Step hard into a strong stance at the same time you snap your wrist.

Double Rising Block Escape from a Choke

Double rising block can help you escape from a choke—*if* you do it well and at the right time. This one works best if you do it before your attacker gets hold of your neck. If a big, strong attacker already has hold of you, chances are hitting their arms with your blocks won't get you loose. If that happens, ducking out and windmill are better choices. But if you see them reaching for you and you can act before it's too late, double rising block might do the job.

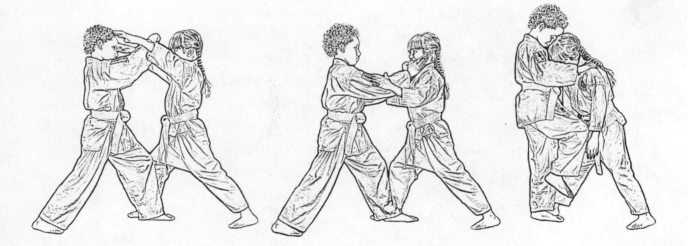

■ TIPS:

Be sure to step into a strong forward stance at the same time as you block to make your block stronger. Once you've done a fast, strong double rising block, *immediately* do double vertical chops to the attacker's collarbones, then follow up with a knee kick. You don't need to keep pushing against the attacker's arms after you've done your block. Remember, you want to break out and finish quickly, so you can run away.

Form—Kata—Poomse

Do you know what *kata* or *poomse* is? *Kata* is the Japanese word and *poomse* is the Korean word for "form" or "pattern." We'll use the English word *form*. A form in martial arts is a series of movements—stances, blocks, strikes, and turns. You must learn the moves, memorize them, and practice the entire series, from beginning to end, many times over—until you can do them quickly, powerfully, and without thinking. Your form should be practiced as though you're fighting off imaginary attackers coming at you from all sides. Practicing this way will help you to be "ready in every direction."

Forms practice is *mental* practice as well as *physical* practice. Besides having to use your mind to memorize the pattern, you must learn to focus, concentrate, and ignore all distractions in order to perform smoothly and without hesitating. Forms practice makes you better at your techniques and turns, and it also helps train your mind and body to work together as one. This is an important skill for self-defense. It's valuable any time you need to act quickly under pressure, including when you're scared. This is a very important part of traditional martial arts training.

Each form begins and ends with a bow. Between bows, you give your complete attention and absolute best effort to your form and nothing but your form. It should feel as though you are the only person in the room, and your form is the only thing in the world.

KIAI! KIHAP!

You probably learned about *kiai* or *kihap* on your very first day of class. It's the shout let out by martial artists when they punch, kick, block, or sometimes just when they step into a stance, ready for action. We often say it means "spirit yell," and that's a pretty good definition. You yell to show your spirit—to let your opponents know you're fierce and ready to defend yourself—and maybe to scare them away. You also yell to *raise* your spirit—in case you're tired or afraid and need to give yourself courage.

A more accurate definition for the words is *harmonizing* or *focusing energy.* The shout teaches you to focus all the power of your mind, your body, and your breath into each technique to make it as strong as it can possibly be. Your shout should come from deep within your belly (not from your mouth or throat), and you should let out all your breath and tighten your stomach muscles when you shout. The breath, the tight muscles, and the loud sound should all come exactly together at the very end of your technique—the very instant when you strike your target or hit your stance.

Once you have memorized a form, practicing it becomes like meditation. If you do it well, you'll hardly remember what you did or how long it took.

Taikyoku and Tae Geuk

Different schools and styles practice different forms. They all practice for the same reasons, though, and the forms they teach to new students often share a lot in common.

Many karate schools, and even a few taekwondo schools, start out with a form called *Taikyoku*. Taikyoku uses 90-degree turns, 180-degree turns, and 270-degree turns, along with basic stances, blocks, and strikes that every beginning martial artist learns.

Many taekwondo schools teach a series of forms called *Tae Geuk*. The first Tae Geuk form also uses those turns and similar basic techniques.

The names *Taikyoku* (Japanese) and *Tae Geuk* (Korean) have the same original meaning. Both are based on the Chinese *taiji*, which is sometimes translated as meaning "the great ultimate." *Tae Geuk* is translated as "great eternity"—that is, something with no beginning, middle, or end, like a universe that contains everything. *Taikyoku* is often translated as "first principle" or "first cause." The *first cause* is what makes everything else happen—it's the source of everything.

If your beginning form is named for *the source of everything*, then forms practice must be very important. You should take it seriously.

Kiai

■ TIPS:

Don't say *kiai!* or *kihap!* when you shout. That would be like yelling by saying *yell!* Instead, make a yell that doesn't say anything. Throw a sound at your opponent the way you might throw a rock. Do you feel shy about yelling in front of others? Everybody does at first. But it's an important skill. So when your teacher says *shout!* just go for it along with all your classmates. Like everything, it will get easier with practice.

Patience and Practice

Learning your first form is challenging. It's important to learn it from your instructor, not from a book. Once you have begun to learn it, you should practice as often as you can. Then, later, use the book for reminders.

At first it's hard to remember when to turn, which way to turn, or which foot to turn with. You might get confused and frustrated and even want to give up. Later you might feel as though you know the form, only to make a big mistake right in the middle. Sometimes it's hard to practice when you don't know if you're doing it right. But practice is the only way to get better.

It's okay to make mistakes; you can always fix them with more practice! It's okay to get mixed up sometimes and even to feel frustrated. But don't give up! Keep at it for as long as it takes to master it—even if it seems like it's going to take forever.

Your instructor will help you with the parts that are hard and give you tips on how to remember what to do. Sometimes your instructor will stop giving you help and will just say to practice and try your best. And that's what you should do.

Build-It-Yourself Taikyoku

Do you remember Gichin Funakoshi? We read about him in Chapter One. Funakoshi created Taikyoku kata to help beginners, and especially young people, get a solid foundation in their martial arts training. In a way Taikyoku is *simple*. It only has a few building blocks, and they're all things you've already learned and practiced. If you've mastered the building blocks, you should be able to put the form together from a set of instructions—just the way you might put together a Lego structure from five or six different kinds of blocks. Try it! (But don't be surprised if it's harder than it sounds.)

This exercise is fun to do with a friend, so one of you can read the instructions, and the other one can try to put it together. It's especially useful if your instructor has already started teaching you this kata in class. If there's a different form your instructor would rather you practice, read this section, then skip ahead to Things to Do.

Here are the building blocks. Each block actually combines more than one element—for example, a stance plus a hand technique, or a step or turn plus a stance plus a hand technique. We've included the pages where the techniques are shown, in case you need to review:

[1] 90-degree turn into forward stance with lower block, page 99 (lower block is on page 68)

[2] Step forward with lunge punch in forward stance, page 65

[3] 180-degree turn into forward stance with lower block, page 100

[4] 270-degree turn into forward stance with lower block, page 101

You also have to know how to bow, because you bow at the beginning and again at the end. You must know natural stance or ready stance, because (as always) we begin and end in that stance. You have to know *kiai* or *kihap*, because it's used twice in the form. And remember the compass we imagined on the floor when you were learning the turns? It would be handy to use that here.

Attention. Bow. Ready stance facing north on your imaginary compass.

[1] *(step left with your left foot)* → [2] →

[3] → [2] →

[1] → [2] → [2] → [2], *shout!*

→ [4] → [2] →

[3] → [2] →

[1] → [2] → [2] → [2], *shout!*

→ [4] → [2] →

[3] → [2] → return 90 degrees, drawing your front foot back to ready stance.

Attention. Bow.

If all went well, you're back where you started, facing "north" in ready stance.

Things to Do

Answers are on page 114.

1. Name these techniques.

Do you remember the names for what these students are practicing? Write them under the pictures.

_____   _____

2. What's wrong with this picture?

This student is trying to do the windmill escape. He's pushing really hard on his partner's arms, but it isn't working. What's he doing wrong? (Hint: Reread the tips on page 92.) Write your answer here:

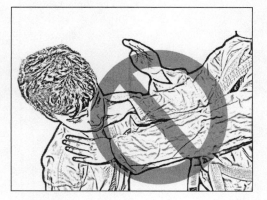

_____

_____

3. Which turn is he doing?

Warning: This puzzle is tricky! Before you start, go back to page 98 and review the four turns and their names. It's okay to stand up and do the turns while you're solving the puzzle. Better yet, do it with a friend so one can do the turn while the other sees how it looks. One more tip: The first and third choices are easy to mix up with each other. So are the second and fourth.

Draw a line from the name of the turn to the correct ending position or write the correct answer in the space provided.

If he starts in this position:

And does this turn:

He'll end in . . . which position?

Reverse

90-degree turn

180-degree turn

270-degree turn

4. Basic training: turns practice.

Add some techniques—blocks and strikes—when you're practicing your turns. Imagine you're turning as quickly as you can to face an opponent; block their attack, and then counterattack. Start by doing each of the four turns in forward stance, ending with a lower block and a reverse punch. Are you in a good, balanced stance when you finish each turn? Can you do a strong block and punch without wobbling? Now see if you can do the same turns in walking stance. Add any techniques you like at the end of the turn.

5. Try this at home: Marbles and Toes.

You'll need a bag of marbles, some empty cups or other containers of different sizes, and a shallow baking pan or some other way to contain the marbles when you pour them onto the floor. (A hula hoop works, too.) Now you have to get all the marbles from the baking pan into the cups—without using your hands. Pick them up with your toes and drop them into the cups. There are three levels of Marbles and Toes:

- **Beginner:** Sit on the floor while using your feet to move the marbles. Hands off!

- **Intermediate:** Stand on one foot while using the other foot to move the marbles. Be sure to try some with each foot.

- **Expert:** Put the cups on your bed. Lift the marbles from the floor and drop them into the cups on your bed. Remember, no hands!

Count your marbles before and after the game, so you don't leave any loose on the floor.

Besides being fun, this is a great way to practice getting your feet and toes to do what you want. (Martial artists need to be able to do that, especially for kicking.) It also improves balance. Expert level works the muscles you use for kicking.

ANSWERS:

Name these techniques. The student on the left is doing lower block. You can tell it's a block and not a low punch because it ends over his leg, not in the center. The student on the right is doing an inner chop—it looks like he's practicing *shifting* chops. **What's wrong with this picture?** He should have raised his arm up high, instead of pushing on the arm. For windmill, he needs to spin his whole arm over the top, using his whole body to twist free. Pushing won't work against some-one big and strong. **Which turn is he doing?** Reverse—4. 90-degree turn—3. 180-degree turn—2. 270-degree turn—1.

LEVEL FOUR

Partner Work Intensive

Practicing with partners—we call it partner work—is fun, and the best thing about it is you can learn things you can't learn by yourself and practice things you can't practice by yourself.

You have probably already done lots of partner work in class. You used it when you practiced choke escapes and thumb escapes. You might also have used partner work to practice your blocks against strikes. Maybe you used a partner to aim at when practicing kicks.

Even though it's fun, partner work can also be challenging. And it gets more and more challenging the higher you go through the belt levels in martial arts. At this level, before we go on to our new techniques and drills, let's talk about doing a good job at partner work.

Etiquette for Practicing with Partners

You already know the first rule of etiquette for practicing with a partner. Write it here: What must you and your partner always do before you begin practicing together?

_____

Why? What does it mean?

_____

Here are some other important things to remember when your instructor has asked you to practice with a partner:

115

1. **Only practice what your instructor told you to practice.** Don't start doing other things just because they might be fun or interesting.

2. **Keep practicing until your instructor asks you to stop,** even if that means doing the same thing over and over, hundreds of times!

3. **Avoid talking or goofing around with your partners.** This is disrespectful to your teacher and classmates and keeps you and your partners from learning.

4. **Try your best and let your partners try their best.** Concentrate on your job and don't try to teach your partners (that's your instructor's job). If you aren't sure what to do, ask your instructor.

5. **Avoid doing anything that might hurt your partners.** If you're supposed to grab, grab firmly but without squeezing. If you're supposed to kick or punch, aim carefully, but be sure you don't actually strike your partner! Move slowly, and only speed up if your teacher asks you to. Remember, your partners could do something unexpected and you might hit them by accident. *Partner work requires great care!*

6. **Make it easy for your partners to practice and learn.** For example, don't kick or punch faster than they can handle. If they're trying to learn to use a block to deflect a punch, you'll need to punch slowly at first, and they'll need to do the same for you. If they're trying to escape from a grab, you shouldn't try to keep them from escaping—you should let them practice their escaping technique to get better at it. And they should do the same for you.

When you bow to your partners before practicing together, you're telling them you respect them and will follow the rules of etiquette when you practice. When you bow to your partners after finishing practice, you're thanking them for their effort and their respect.

What to Do If Your Partner Makes Mistakes

One hard thing about partner work is that you and your partner are both trying to learn something new. That means there are going to be mistakes. *Everyone* is going to make mistakes.

Sometimes it feels as though you can't practice right because your partner keeps messing up. When that happens—before you get impatient or start telling your partner what to do—slow down and remember the rules of etiquette. Are *you* trying *your* best? Are you doing your job the best you can possibly do? Are you making it easy for your partner to practice and learn? Do you need to ask the instructor for help?

Most of the time, both partners are making mistakes, even when one partner thinks it's the other one's fault. That's just the way people are! And that's the way learning is. Everyone has to make a lot of mistakes in order to master worthwhile skills. There's a lot you can learn even when making mistakes. So no matter what happens, find a way to keep doing your best.

The important thing is to practice! Let's try out your partner work skills on a new exercise.

Blocks & Punches with a Partner

"Blocks & Punches" is the name of a fun, challenging partner exercise. It lets you practice your blocks against punches and practice punching toward a partner. If you want to be good at it, you'll have to concentrate, and you and your partner will have to work well together. It takes a lot of patience to get it just right.

The Starting Position:

Two partners face each other in rectangular stance. One is going to punch—she has her left fist out toward her partner as if she just did a left low punch. Her right fist is on her side ready to punch. The other partner is going to block. He has his arms in position, ready

HAVE YOU SEEN THESE PARTNERS?

The instructor calls out, "Get a partner!" In martial arts classes all over the country, serious young students hear this command, turn to each other, bow to the nearest classmate, and begin practicing.

But—wait! Who are *those* people? They look familiar, because you'll find them in every school:

- There's "Best Friends Only." Every time, he runs to his best friend and starts pulling on his arm—even if he already has another partner.

- There's "I Like *Her* Better." You start to bow to each other, but then someone walks up, and he turns his back and bows to her instead!

- There's "The Runner." He sees you coming and keeps moving away, around and around the room, trying to find someone else—*anyone* else—to go with.

- There's the "Boy-Girl Police"—trying to make sure boys go only with boys and girls go only with girls. And if they end up with members of the opposite sex, they roll their eyes and maybe even sulk!

- Then there's "Eyes to the Ceiling." This student just stands there looking at the ceiling while everyone else is finding partners. He then raises his hand and says, "I don't have a partner." Sometimes there are two of them standing side by side, both raising their hands, and both saying, "I don't have a partner."

Have you seen these partners? Have you *been* one of these partners? Let's hope not, because each of them is showing bad manners and disrespect. In martial arts class, everyone must respect everyone equally. Each student must be willing and able to practice with any other student—showing equal good manners to all. If you favor some and avoid others, you're showing disrespect.

"Eyes to the Ceiling" might have a different problem. He might be shy or afraid of having his feelings hurt if no one will be his partner. That's understandable—but even so he still has to look for a partner. If the teacher says to find a partner and you don't even try, you're showing disrespect to the teacher *and* your classmates.

Good etiquette demands that when you hear the command "find a partner," you turn to the nearest classmate—*no matter who they are*—bow, and practice. If the person nearest you is "taken," move quickly to the next available person. If there's an odd number and you end up alone, quickly join a pair to make a group of three.

Try not to go with the same people all the time. You'll learn more by practicing with all kinds of different partners. Try to go with bigger people, smaller people, younger and older, more advanced and less advanced, boys, girls—just try everybody! And above all, treat everybody with respect.

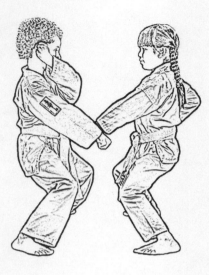

to do a lower block with his left arm. That is, he's in the "load" position for left lower block. (Where should his left fist be? Hint: See page 68.)

The Puncher's Job:

The puncher will do good, straight punches toward the blocker, starting with a right low punch. She'll do four low punches in a row (right, left, right, left), then continue with four middle punches (right, left, right, left), then continue with four high punches toward his nose (right, left, right, left). She'll punch slowly and carefully, never going faster than the blocker can handle.

The Blocker's Job:

The blocker will block each punch, catching it on the side of the arm as it comes in and deflecting it just far enough, so it would miss him if it kept coming. He'll start with lower blocks in this order—pay attention, this is the tricky part: *left, right, right, left.* Then he'll do inner middle blocks, left, right, right, left; then rising blocks, left, right, right, left. (Our illustrations only show lower block. You'll have to do the rest yourself!)

Tips for the Puncher:

Remember your reaction hand: When you punch with one fist, pull the other one back to your side, ready to punch. This way, you'll never get mixed up about which hand punches next. Always start in the correct starting position, and make sure your partner is ready before you throw the first punch.

Tips for the Blocker:

Don't get thrown off by having someone in front of you punching at you. Just do the same good blocks you always practice. Remember to load for every block! The pictures show the load positions, because they're so important. Block using the side of the arm, not the back of the arm. Remind yourself (silently) as you go, saying, *left, right, right, left; left, right, right, left. . . .* You can practice the pattern by yourself with an imaginary partner. It's fun to do it in front of a mirror.

Tips for Everyone:

This exercise is really hard! You'll make many, many mistakes and sometimes feel very confused. Don't be discouraged. Keep practicing, and you'll get better and better at it.

Why do you think we block left, right, right, left instead of left, right, left, right?

If you can't think of an answer, practice with your classmates and talk it over. If you still can't think of an answer, ask your teachers and see what they think.

If your school has a different blocking and punching exercise your teacher wants you to practice, be sure you practice that one first!

Now let's look at some new techniques for Level Four.

Hand Techniques

Double Punch
(morote-zuki, du jumŏk chirŭgi)

This is easy: two punches at the same time! Make sure they're both good, strong punches and are done correctly. That means your fists must start on your sides, palms up. Keep your elbows close to your sides as the punches come out. Twist both fists, palms down, at the end of the punch. Your two fists should be close together at the end, about an inch apart.

High-Low Double Punch

Could you have guessed this technique just by the name? Think about it. It's two punches at the same time—just like double punch—but one is aimed high and one is aimed low. Make sure one punch is right below the other.

Double Inner Middle Block

You already know inner middle block. (Do you remember the name in Japanese, in Korean? See page 81 for a reminder and write it under the picture, with *double—morote* or *du*.) You can probably figure out how to do double inner middle block. What would be the correct starting position?

Outer Chop
(soto shuto-uchi, son-nal jechyo chigi)

Remember inner chop? It starts on the inside (near one ear) and moves to the outside. Outer chop starts on the outside (behind the outside ear) and chops across in front of you. It's done as if you were slicing the top off something using the knife-edge of your hand.

■ TIPS:

To get ready, raise your arm high enough to put your hand behind your head and push your elbow back. Don't forget your reaction hand: Thrust it out in front toward your opponent, and when you chop, pull the reaction hand back to your side at the same time.

Shifting Outer Chop

In this exercise, instead of pulling the reaction hand back to your side, leave it up high and hidden behind your head. (Hide your weapon!) A person standing right in front of you shouldn't be able to see your elbow sticking out from behind your head. This will help you practice good posture and body alignment for getting the most from your outer chop. (You may also want to practice pulling your reaction hand to your side.)

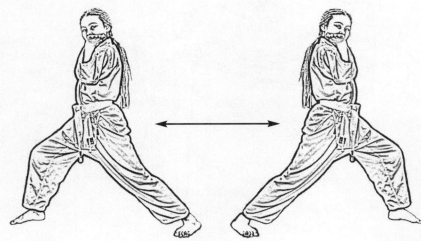

Leg Techniques

Front Thrust Kick
(mae-geri-kekomi, ap jillo chagi)

This kick is a lot like stomping on something—but stomping forward, instead of stomping down on the ground. It's very important to raise your knee high for this kick. You'll strike the target with your *heel.*

■ TIPS:

Pull your foot up tight—it shouldn't be loose and floppy. Pick your knee up high! After you strike the (real or imaginary) target, pull your knee back up before putting your foot down. Don't just let your foot fall to the floor after you kick; place it down deliberately—in position for a good stance.

Escaping Techniques

Third Thumb Escape

This is for grab #3, which is _____.

It combines movements from the first and second thumb escapes. When you step to the dead side, one hand will go to the opposite-side ear—ready for inner chop—and the other hand will break out with a motion similar to inner middle block. Snap both hands into position hard and fast as you step.

Does it matter which side you step to? _____.

Be sure to practice both sides, in case you're in a situation where you don't get to choose. Can you think of a situation when it would matter which way you stepped?

■ TIPS:

If you step to the right, both hands go toward your left shoulder. If you step to the left, both hands go to the _____. You may use either hand to jam the attacker's arm. Then immediately use the other hand to strike (chop or punch), and follow up with a knee kick.

Fourth Thumb Escape

This is for breaking out of grab #4. Which grab is that? _____.
On grab #4, both thumbs are on top. So where does your arm have
to go in order to break out? _____.

■ TIPS:

Don't play tug of war with your arm! If you pull on your arm, the
attacker—who might be bigger and stronger than you are—will pull
back. Instead of pulling back or pulling up, bend your knees and
lower your elbow underneath the attacker's hands. Then you can
use your legs and your whole body to rise up and break free against
the thumbs. As you rise up, pretend you're drawing a stripe up the
middle of your attacker using the tip of your elbow. Be careful not
to hit your partner in the chin with your elbow accidentally when
you are practicing. Your elbow is a powerful weapon and you could
hurt someone. That's why it's so useful for self-defense—when you
really need it.

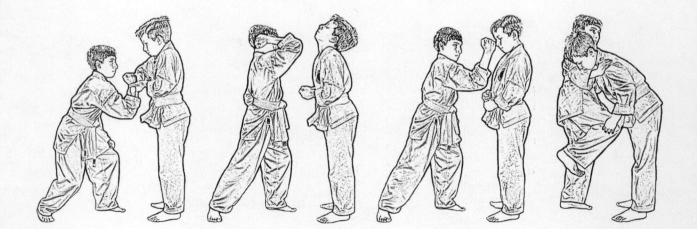

Form—Kata—Poomse

By now you should know at least one form very well. Whether it's Taikyoku, Tae Geuk El-jang, or a different form entirely, you should have practiced it many times. You should know the moves without thinking. You should be able to perform with power and focus.

Once you know your first form very well—you still keep practicing it! Even after you learn a second, third, or many more forms, you'll still keep practicing all of them. Advanced black belts still practice Taikyoku. There's always something you can make better about your performance. There's always something deeper to understand about your moves.

Modified Forms

Modified means "changed." If you truly know and understand your form, you won't get confused even if the instructor asks you to change something about it—for example, by performing it using different blocks or strikes, or moving backward instead of forward. Or you could do the whole form in mirror image.

Mirror image is pretty hard! Let's start with something easier. Try modifying one of the blocks you use in your form. For example, if you practice Taikyoku, wherever you would usually do a lower block in the form, do a middle block instead. Leave everything else the same.

The next time through, substitute rising block—or maybe double rising block—for lower block. Also try modifying the stance—for example, doing Taikyoku in walking stance instead of forward stance.

If you practice a form other than Taikyoku, think about how you could modify your kata. How could you keep the *pattern* the same but change some of the *techniques?* This will deepen your understanding of your form and give you another way to practice your techniques.

Things to Do

(Answers are on page 130.)

1. Name the techniques.

These two pictures go together. In the first picture, one student is grabbing the other student's wrist with grab # ____. What technique are they practicing together? Write it underneath.

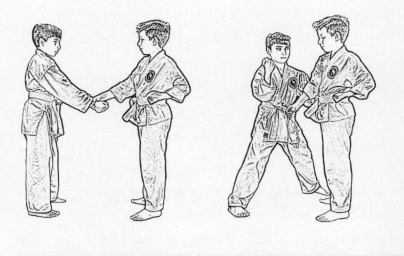

Why is it called a thumb escape? Circle the letter for the right answer:

a. Because you use your thumb to escape with.

b. Because you pull on your attacker's thumb in order to escape.

c. Because your attacker grabbed you by the thumb, and you escape.

d. Because you escape by breaking out against your opponent's thumb.

2. Which rising block would you use—and why?

Here are five rising blocks. You have seen most of them before. Do you remember which ones are making big mistakes? Put a star next to the good one(s). On the bad ones, circle the part that's wrong and write what's wrong underneath. If you need help, review the tips on page 69.

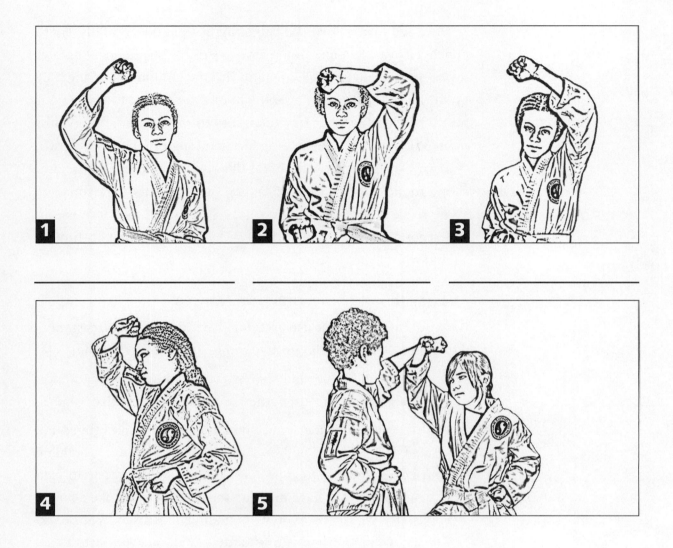

3. Basic training: ball toss.

For this practice session, you'll need a playground ball—the kind used to play dodgeball or four square. It can be small or medium-sized. You'll use the ball to practice aim, focus, and timing.

Hold the ball with one hand, extended out in front of you. Now try to punch it away with your other fist. If your punch is straight, focused, and on target, the ball will shoot away from you in a straight line. Practice to get it straighter and farther.

Now add *timing*. Toss the ball straight up, and as it falls, try to punch it in a straight line. You'll have to strike at just the right instant! If you're knocking the ball down toward the ground or making it fly up in the air, you're hitting too late or too early—or maybe your punch is just going wild! Stay calm, concentrate, and try to get it just right. Make sure you're standing in a good stance when you punch.

Try practicing other techniques this way, too: inner chops, outer chops, roundhouse kicks, even blocks. But first make sure you have a safe space where it's okay to send a ball flying! Ask permission, and of course, be careful not to hit the ball into the street or through a window.

4. Try this at home: practical stances.

Did you know you can use and practice your martial arts stances when doing ordinary, day-to-day things? Here are two examples:

1. You can tie and untie your shoe while standing in kicking stance. This is a great way to strengthen your legs and practice balance.

2. You can use rectangular stance when you have to pick things up: Instead of bending over, drop low by stepping wide and bending your knees, keeping good posture. Lift by using your legs instead of your back. If you have to lift up something heavy, like a box of books, this will protect you from pulling a muscle in your back. But you can practice this technique any time, even just to pick up a pencil.

ANSWERS:

Name the techniques. It's grab #2—opposite-side wrist grab—and they're practicing the second thumb escape. **Why is it called thumb escape?** D. **Which rising block would you use?** Numbers 3 and 5 are both good. Don't use number 1, because it isn't protecting the whole head. Number 2 is too flat and close to the head. So is number 4, plus her wrist is bent—not correct and not very strong!

Stances and Strategy

You've learned many different stances. As a beginner, most of your practice is in forward stance or walking stance. When you move up and down the room doing blocks, kicks, and strikes, you're probably in one of those two stances. Both stances help you practice good posture and balance. Both stances face your opponent head-on, so it's easy to see where to block and strike—even when it's an imaginary attacker.

Every stance has different advantages. Walking stance is comfortable and easy to learn. It lets you move easily in any direction. Forward stance has stability and strength. It helps you use the power of your legs and hips.

There are other ways of standing and moving that a good martial artist needs to know. In a fight you might not always want to face your opponent head-on; there are other strategies, or plans of action, you might want to try. You might want to move around quickly, so no one can take aim. You might want to protect your body but still be ready to kick. You might want to be able to fight back while *retreating* (moving away).

Good martial artists want many choices. They need to be ready for anything, and that means having different strategies—and stances—for different situations. Let's look at some new ones.

Stances

Cat or Tiger Stance
(neko-ashi-dachi, beom sogi)

This stance is suitable for lightning-quick movements like springing out of the way, springing back at your opponent, or kicking suddenly without warning. To get into cat stance, turn one foot sideways and put the other foot in front like a *T*. Then slide that foot forward a little bit. Sink down with all your weight on your back foot, and let your front foot touch the floor lightly with just the ball of the foot, or in some styles, the tip of the toe.

In some schools and styles, cat stance is lower and longer—there's more space between the feet, and you crouch down more on your back leg. Which way do you do it at your school?

Since all your weight is on your back foot, you can lift up your front foot really easily. Why is that a handy thing to be able to do? Think about it.

When you move forward and backward in cat stance, you move on a zigzag line, not a straight line. Each step is like a little hop, as though you were springing back and forth over a rope. (That's a good way to practice. We'll try it later on.)

■ TIPS:

Whether you're going forward or backward, lead the way with your front foot (the one you can lift up easily). Spring forward (or back) and land with all your weight on that foot, then bring the other foot in front. You'll switch stances with each step. Can you do 90-degree turn, 180-degree turn, 270-degree turn, and reverse in cat stance? If you can't figure out how, ask your instructor for help.

Side Stance

This is a horse stance, or straddle-leg stance, turned sideways. (Do you remember the Japanese and Korean names? Look on page 57 and write them under the picture.) In side stance only your head and eyes are facing forward. It's harder for your opponent to attack your body, but you can still defend yourself and strike back. There are many ways to move in side stance. Start with stepping forward (like walking, but ending sideways with each step) and turning behind (turning your back as you step). Both ways can *advance* or *retreat.*

■ TIPS:

When stepping forward or back in side stance, don't swing your foot wide as if you're turning on a circle. Slide it along a straight line, right past your other foot. Can you do 90-degree turn, 180-degree turn, 270-degree turn, and reverse in side stance? (Hint: On reverse, you don't even need to move your feet!)

Hand Techniques

Here's a nice, quick punch to go with cat stance:

Vertical Punch
(tate-zuki, sewo chirŭgi)

Remember the very first punch you learned? It was called horizontal punch. Later you learned horizontal chop and vertical chop. What does "horizontal" mean?

_____

_____

What does "vertical" mean? _____
Why is a vertical chop called "vertical"?

_____

(See page 80 to review.)
Unlike vertical chop, vertical punch isn't vertical because it starts up high and goes down. It's called "vertical" because your fist is in a vertical position (knuckles up and down) at the end of the punch. Thrust straight out and only twist your fist halfway.

   How would you do a double vertical punch?

_____

(See page 122 if you need a hint.)

Horizontal Backfist
(uraken-uchi, tŭngjumŏk chigi)

Start, or load, as though you were going to do an inner middle block. Then swing your fist up to strike head level. Keep a tight fist and strike with the back of the knuckles.

■ TIPS:

This strike can also start at your ear, like inner chop (see page 66). And it's a great strike to practice while moving in side stance, especially with the turning behind step. Most of the time you should aim your backfist head level, as though striking the side of the head.

Don't be fooled:

Horizontal backfist gets its name because it moves horizontally (side to side). But it has a vertical fist at the end! Don't let this confuse you.

Vertical Backfist
(tate uraken-uchi, naeryo tŭngjumŏk chigi)

It starts the same as horizontal backfist, but circles up and over and strikes down. Imagine hitting the top of your opponent's nose. Why is it called "vertical" backfist?

Outer Middle Block
(soto ude-uke, ahn jung dan makgi)

Sometimes we just call it outer block. Compare this one to inner middle block. Why do you think this new one is called *outer* middle block?

Compare it to outer chop. What do the two have in common?

■ TIPS:

Remember your reaction hand every time you block! Be sure to block far enough across in front of your body to keep a punch from hitting you. And don't forget to twist your forearm right at the end of the block. What part of your arm should strike the punch as it comes in?

Leg Techniques

Side Thrust Kick
(yoko-geri-kekomi, yop-jillo chagi)

With enough practice, this might become your most powerful kick. If you're starting in side stance, raise your front knee to belt level, then thrust straight out. If you're starting in forward stance, you'll need to bring your knee all the way around to sideways as you raise it, then thrust it out.

■ TIPS:

Strike with the knife-edge of the foot. Some schools also emphasize striking with the heel. Avoid pointing your toes or letting the front part of your foot hit the target first. That could jam your toes or your ankle! For the most powerful kick, it's important to use your hips, not just your leg. Don't try to keep your body facing toward the target. Let it face the side as you thrust your hip and leg all the way out straight. The foot you're standing on will point away from the target at the end of the kick.

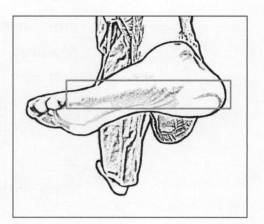

Blocks & Punches with a Partner

Try adding the outer block to your Blocks & Punches exercise. After you complete the set of four rising blocks, the puncher will punch another four times to the middle, and the blocker will do four outer middle blocks. Which arm blocks first?

_____

What order do you block in? (What's the blocking pattern for Blocks & Punches?)

_____

Do you have to use your reaction hand on all four blocks?

_____

True or false: The puncher punches right, left, left, right.

_____

(See page 120 for the answer.)

If you're good at doing the exercise in rectangular stance, try it moving forward and backward in walking stance or forward stance!

Escaping Techniques

Fifth Thumb Escape

In grab #5, where is your attacker standing? If your hands are being held behind your back, you're in a bad spot. The first thing to do is get your hands in front of your hips. Back up and bump into your attacker if necessary. Then you can proceed with your escape.

■ TIPS:

When you move to break out, drop your elbows down toward your attacker's arms. Move fast and hard—never do it halfway! Step into a long, strong forward stance to add power to your escape. Once you're free, you can do *reverse* in forward stance, and follow up with a chop, punches, and kicks. Or better yet, what else could you do, once you break free? (Reread page 87 if you need a hint.)

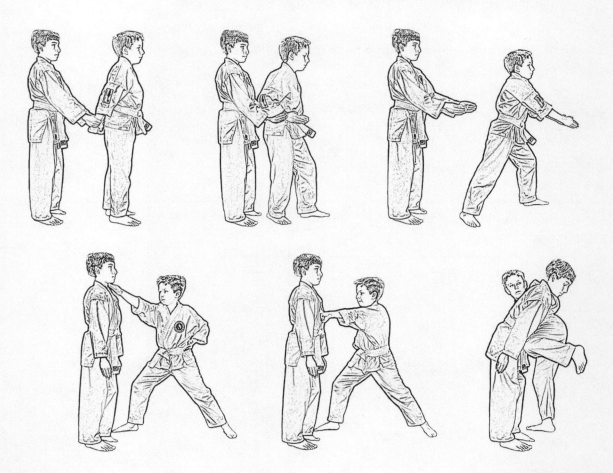

Form—Kata—Poomse

Remember when we learned about modified forms? If you understand your form well enough, you'll be able to change things about it without getting confused. Learning a new form isn't really that different from practicing a modified form. The better you know your first form, the easier it will be to learn new forms.

In many schools and styles, all the forms you'll learn early on share a basic pattern in common. For example, the Taikyoku series of katas have the shape of a capital letter *I*. The Pinan or Heian series of katas, taught in many karate schools, start with that basic capital-*I* pattern and modify it in different ways as the katas become more advanced.

The Tae Geuk series of poomsae all share the same basic pattern, too. (If you practice the Tae Geuk forms, see if you can draw a picture of that pattern.) Think of each new form you learn as a modified version of the last one.

The key to learning new katas is to make sure you know the building blocks. Then learn to fit the blocks together smoothly. Finally, practice until you can perform from beginning to end without thinking. And when you can do that—practice some more!

Modified Form with Snap Kicks and Thrust Kicks

Here's a modified version of Taikyoku that uses front *snap* kicks and front *thrust* kicks. It uses *consecutive* punches (lunge punch-reverse punch, one right after the other) and *double* punches (two at the same time). It also uses inner horizontal chop. Make sure you remember Taikyoku before you try to follow these instructions (and if there's a different form your instructor would prefer you practice—do that instead!):

1. Wherever you'd normally do lower block, do inner chop instead.

2. Wherever you'd step forward with lunge punch once in a row, instead do this combination: front snap kick, lunge punch-reverse punch.

HOW GOOD ARE YOUR PUSH-UPS?

Some students love them. Some hate them. They're a favorite with martial arts instructors. You're going to have to do a lot of push-ups. Are you doing a good job?

Lots of kids say push-ups are easy. They say they can do fifty or even a hundred. Lots of times, they aren't exactly telling the truth. They might be *counting* to fifty or a hundred, but their arms aren't really doing that many pushups, and their bodies aren't really holding the right position.

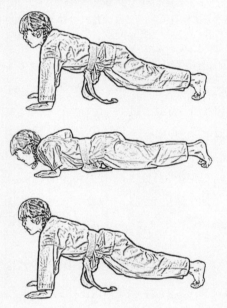

A good push-up means you're holding your body straight, you're bending your arms at the elbow, and you're going all the way down till you *almost* touch the floor, then all the way back up.

Some people do "sag-downs" instead of push-ups. That's when your body sags down, then wiggles up and down a little bit. Your elbows don't bend very much, either. Some people do "bobble-heads" instead of push-ups. That's when your head hangs down, you bobble it up and down, and your elbows don't bend very much.

Don't do sag-downs—they're bad for your back!

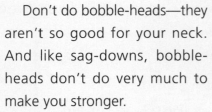

Don't do bobble-heads—they aren't so good for your neck. And like sag-downs, bobble-heads don't do very much to make you stronger.

Be honest: It's hard work to do excellent push-ups. Even kids who are really good at them are working hard. Take the trouble to work hard and try your best. If your teacher says to do five push-ups, but you can't really do five excellent push-ups, then do what you can:

- If you can't do one excellent push-up, then start by just holding yourself up in push-up position for as long as you can. Tighten up your stomach muscles and don't sag or bobble! You can practice this any time, even while watching TV.

- If you can't do five but you can do one or two, then do the one or two and try to add another each time you practice. If you can't do twenty, but you can do ten—same thing.

- If you can't do good push-ups on the floor, start by doing them against a wall. Try the floor again when you feel stronger.

- Practice every day and do your best every time. You'll get stronger more quickly by practicing consistently.

Don't worry if you have a hard time with push-ups, when other kids find it easy. People are different. Different people struggle with different things. Just do your absolute best and work to get better.

3. Wherever you'd normally step forward with lunge punch three times in a row, instead do this combination three times in a row: front thrust kick, double punch. (Don't forget the *shout* on the third double punch!)

This form will test your mastery of certain techniques. It asks you to:

- Know and show the difference between front snap kick and front thrust kick.

- Know and show the difference between lunge punch and reverse punch.

- Know and show the difference between consecutive punches and double punches.

Here are some tips:

- Keep tight fists when you're getting ready for double punch (and for all your punches).

- When doing your front thrust kick, remember to pull both fists all the way back to your ribs, palms up, ready to do a double punch.

- Don't forget to pull your knee back up after the front thrust kick, so you can step forward (instead of falling forward) into a good stance.

Things to Do

(Answers are on page 147.)

1. Name the techniques.

Can you recognize these load positions? Under each picture, write the name of the technique the student is about to do. There may be more than one possible answer.

 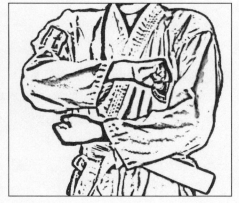

2. What's wrong with this picture?

Everything! Wow. This student is having a really bad day. He's trying his best, but he's making a lot of mistakes. Maybe he's trying to do a punch, but it's not clear. Circle as many mistakes as you can find (there are at least five).

3. Connect the name with the picture.

For each numbered technique there is a corresponding picture. Write the number in the space next to the picture.

1. Vertical Chop _____

2. Horizontal Backfist _____

3. Vertical Punch _____

4. Horizontal Punch _____

5. Vertical Backfist _____

4. Basic training: the rope.

Remember how cat stance moves in a zigzag line, like hopping back and forth over a rope? It's time to practice. Stretch out a rope on some flat ground where there's room to practice. Near one end of the rope, stand with the rope on your left, in left cat stance, with your left foot angled toward the rope. Now, work your way to the other end of the rope: Lift your left knee, kick over the rope, then hop over and land in *right* cat stance. Next lift your right knee, kick over the rope, hop over, and land in *left* cat stance. Continue down the length of the rope, then back again—many times over! You may use any kick but start with front snap kick. Then add blocks and strikes at the end of your hop. When you feel confident, try it moving backward: that is, kick *forward* over the rope, then use that same leg to retreat *back* over the rope. Don't get mixed up and land on the same side twice in a row!

5. Try this at home: practicing the five A's.

First: Do you remember the Five A's? Look on page 80 if you need a reminder and write them here:

_____

_____

_____

Good martial artists are always practicing the Five A's. This means that they're always noticing what's around them, keeping an eye out for trouble, and looking for ways to avoid it. It just becomes a habit. The most important part of the habit is the first part: being *aware* and *alert*. This exercise will help you get in the habit.

Next time you take a walk—whether it's walking home from school or a friend's house, going to the park, or walking to the grocery store with your parents—purposely notice certain things, and when you get home, write them down. Do it with a friend and compare your answers. Take out a piece of paper and write down these questions:

- How many people did you see? What were they doing?

  _____

  _____

  _____

- Was anyone wearing anything unusual or acting strangely? If so, describe it.

  _____

  _____

  _____

- Were there places along the way where someone could hide and jump out at you? Is there a way you could safely avoid those places or keep a distance from them?

  _____

  _____

  _____

- Were there any barking dogs or dogs running loose along your route?

  _____

  _____

  _____

- Along your route, was there a friend's house you could go to in case of emergency? Where was it?

  _____

  _____

  _____

- Was there another place you could go in an emergency, like a fire station or store?

_____

_____

_____

- Did you notice anything else that was interesting or unusual?

_____

_____

_____

Don't look just for bad things or dangerous things. Notice positive things, too—like a cool car, interesting plants in a garden, birds and other animals, or the sound of someone practicing the trumpet.

Do this exercise as many times as you like. You'll get better and better at noticing things.

ANSWERS:

Name the techniques. On the left is the load position for right inner middle block. It could also be for double inner middle block or maybe even a backfist strike. On the right is the load position for left rising block. **What's wrong with this picture?** (1) bad posture, (2) bent wrist, (3) reaction hand hanging down, (4) poor fists, and (5) poor stance: the heel is up. And maybe you can find even more things wrong! **Connect the names with the pictures.** (1) d, (2) c, (3) a, (4) e, (5) b.

Practicing the Five A's: Awareness, Alertness, Avoidance, Anticipation, Action.

The Line of Attack and Defense

The *line of attack* is the straight line from the middle of your opponent (or training partner) to the middle of you. If they attack you, for instance, with a punch or kick, it will have to follow that line to get to you. If you counterattack, it's the same thing—you'll follow that line to get to them. Even if you use a technique that doesn't go in a straight line—like a roundhouse kick—it will still start at the beginning of the line (the middle of you) and end at the other end (the middle of them, assuming you hit your target!).

Any time you face a partner, you can imagine the line of attack. Now you know where to put up your defense. You know where the attacks will come from. Of course, your opponent can move around (and so can you). Any time you face a partner, your eyes should be on the line of attack, keeping your opponent in your sights.

In Level Five, about *stances and strategy*, we saw that forward stance faces your opponent head-on. *Head-on* means the whole front of your body is facing the line of attack. That's okay if you have a plan, but it makes it easier for your opponent to attack the front of your body. Part of your *strategy* is deciding how much of your body should face the line of attack.

In cat stance your body was half turned away. It didn't face head-on, even though your front foot was ready to strike on the line of attack. In side stance the whole front of your body was turned aside—much harder for your opponent to get to.

It may sound like both stances are better than forward stance, but there are other parts of strategy, too. For each stance, there are advantages and disadvantages. Listen carefully to your instructors and learn what they think about the different stances and what each one is good for. Now let's look at two more. These two are difficult and will take a lot of practice if you want to do them well.

Stances

Back Stance
(kokutsu-dachi, dwi-gubi sogi)

Start with your feet *perpendicular* and your heels together. (This means your back foot is pointing sideways, and your front foot is pointing straight ahead.) Now slide your front foot forward until your stance is almost as long as a side stance would be. Keep most of the weight (almost three quarters) on your back leg. Your back knee stays almost over your back foot, and your front knee should be slightly bent. Your body is turned at least halfway off the line of attack. Your front foot is right on the line, aiming at your opponent.

■ TIPS:

Don't let your front knee straighten out. If you can't keep it a little bent, maybe your stance is too long. Also be careful not to lean back; keep good posture. When you step forward, don't let your weight go onto your front leg (like forward stance); keep it mostly over your back leg. Be careful not to show the front of your body to your opponent. Check your feet. Are they perpendicular? It takes a lot of care and practice to do back stance well!

Diagonal Stance
(fudo-dachi, sasun sogi)

This is a lot like side stance: Your feet are parallel to each other, both your knees are bent, and your weight is evenly divided over your legs. But something is different: Do you know what *diagonal* means? In side stance you were standing right on the line of attack, completely sideways, with only your head and eyes facing down the line. In diagonal stance you're standing *corner to corner* across the line of attack. (*Diagonal* means corner to corner.) Your body is only half turned from the line. Your head and eyes still face forward.

■ TIPS:

If you start in a correct forward stance, you can shift into a good diagonal stance without moving your feet from their spots. Just *pivot* your feet until they're parallel, and shift your weight until it's even on both feet. If you're in a good diagonal stance, you can shift back into a good forward stance by turning your feet forward and thrusting some of your weight forward onto your front leg while straightening your back leg.

A Powerful Combination:

Switching between diagonal stance and forward stance teaches a lot about using the power of your legs and hips. Try this: Start in left forward stance. Without taking a step, do a left outer block. As your block drops across in front of you, shift your hips and legs into diagonal stance. Now shift back into forward stance while throwing a reverse punch. See how powerful you can make that punch when you push with your rear leg and snap your hips forward! Practice this over and over. It's a great exercise.

Hand Techniques

Knifehand Block
(shuto-uke, son-nal makgi)

The starting position is similar to the start of inner chop. As you block, instead of straightening your arm, drop your elbow down and forward as you rotate your forearm, snapping your knifehand into place. You'll deflect a punch by striking it with the outside edge of your hand. What will the other hand do?

■ TIPS:

Keep a tight hand and tight fingers. Don't bend your wrist! That's probably the hardest part.

Knifehand Block in Back Stance

When you're moving in back stance, your *reaction hand* for knifehand block doesn't pull back to your side. Instead it guards your *solar plexus*—that place just below where your ribs come together and just above your stomach.

When you do *reverse* with back stance knifehand block, instead of reaching forward with your reaction hand, reach back. As you block, be careful not to let your arms drop down and then have to come back up—just snap both hands into place.

■ TIPS:

Be sure you have a good, tight knifehand and straight wrist on your reaction hand. It should be *level*—parallel to the ground. Pretend you're balancing a marble on the palm of your hand: it shouldn't roll off or roll up toward your elbow.

Leg Techniques

Axe Kick
(kakato otoshi geri, naeryo chagi)

For this kick, you swing your foot up high, then let it crash down on its target like an axe. It helps to be flexible to do this kick!

■ TIPS:

You can swing your leg straight up and attack straight ahead or swing it over from one side and then down—inside to outside or outside to inside. Tighten your stomach muscles when you swing your leg up. That will help you keep good posture and balance. If you let your head and shoulders lean back, you might slip and fall over backward!

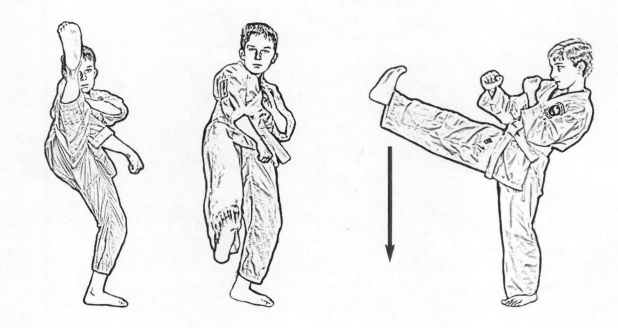

Jumping and Flying Kicks
(tobi-geri, twi-o chagi)

Jumping can sometimes help you add more power to a technique, by springing up into it. It can also help you go farther: You can reach an opponent who is backing up or who is a little too far away to reach with a regular kick. A good jump will get you there quickly and surprise them. It's also just fun!

Let's begin with a jumping upward knee kick. Start in forward stance. As you swing your rear knee up for the kick, use your front leg to push off the ground and spring up into the air. (Once you're in the air, what started as your front leg has now become your rear leg.) Jumping knee kick is preparation for doing jumping kicks of all kinds, like jumping front snap, roundhouse, side kick, and more. Start by working on your jumping skills.

If you really want to fly, do a jumping knee kick, then use the springing leg to do a second knee kick before you land—one-two! You'll go even higher and farther if you take some steps before you jump or take a running start.

■ TIPS:

Control your hands and arms while you're jumping and flying. Don't let them wave around wildly! Try to land in a good stance and throw some punches toward your imaginary opponent. If you can do that, it means you have recovered your balance after landing. Once you're good at flying knee kicks, you can try almost any flying kick.

Blocks & Punches with a Partner

Try adding knifehand block to your Blocks & Punches exercise. Now you have five different blocks in the set. You'll block left-right-right-left using each block in turn:

1. lower block

2. inner middle block

3. rising block

4. outer block

5. knifehand block

Your puncher will do five sets of four punches each, punching right-left-right-left:

1. low punches

2. middle punches

3. high punches

4. middle punches

5. middle punches

If you practice other blocks at your school, add them to the exercise, too!

Escaping Techniques

You've already learned three escapes from a choke and five escapes from wrist grabs. Instead of learning a new one, it's time to review all the old ones and make sure you're doing them correctly.

Can you name your three choke escapes? And add any others you have learned at your school.

1. _____

2. _____

3. _____

_____

_____

_____

Our five escapes from wrist grabs also have a name. They're called _____ escapes. Now write the names of other escapes (if any) you've learned in your school:

_____

_____

_____

Once you're sure you can do all these techniques right—keep practicing! It's always possible to make them better, faster, and stronger.

Form—Kata—Poomse

Now is a good time for you to review the form (or forms) you've learned so far at your school. Pay attention to what your instructor has told you about your forms. If there's one form your instructor thinks you should practice more than the others—that's what you should do. If there's one area he or she wants you to improve—like longer stances, stronger blocks, or better turns—then concentrate on that.

As a dedicated martial artist, you should practice your forms every day, from the first one you learned to the most advanced. If, at the end of a very busy day, you don't have time to practice, try this: As you lie in bed getting ready to sleep, imagine yourself practicing your katas. Be sure to imagine yourself doing strong moves and excellent stances!

Machine Gun Kata

Here's one more version of modified Taikyoku you can practice as an exercise. This one was created by Ngo Dong, the founder of Cuong Nhu karate, to challenge students to do fast combinations—that is, to throw blocks, kicks, and punches—one after the other—as fast as a machine gun would fire its bullets. This form uses three levels of blocks: low, middle, and high. It uses three levels of punches: high, middle, and low. And it uses front snap kick.

Review Taikyoku before trying to follow these instructions:

1. Wherever you would normally do lower block, instead do all three blocks in quick succession (one after the other). Use the same arm on all three blocks. For example, on the first count, you'll turn to your left into left forward stance and do left lower block, left middle block, left rising block—as quickly and powerfully as you can.

2. Wherever you would normally do step forward lunge punch, instead do front snap kick, followed by three punches, three levels (high-middle-low).

3. Wherever you would normally do step forward lunge punch three times in a row, instead do front snap kick quickly three times in a row—and only after the third kick, land in forward stance with three punches, three levels and *shout!*

■ TIPS:

Don't forget to *load* for each and every block! That means using both arms for each block. It's hard work, but no shortcuts are allowed! Whenever you try to perform moves as fast as you possibly can, remember, that really means *as fast as you can do it and still do a good job.* Maybe you won't be as fast as a machine gun right away. It will take practice. It's important to practice doing it *right* first. Then you can do it faster.

Things to Do

(Answers are on page 162.)

1. Name the techniques.

Each of these students is demonstrating a stance. Write the name of the stance below the picture.

_____   _____

2. What's wrong with these pictures?

The pictures show different techniques, but they have a mistake in common. Can you see what it is? Circle it in each picture. The student in #4 is making more than just that one mistake. Do you see the others? If you need a hint, reread the tips for back stance on page 150. Now circle all his mistakes.

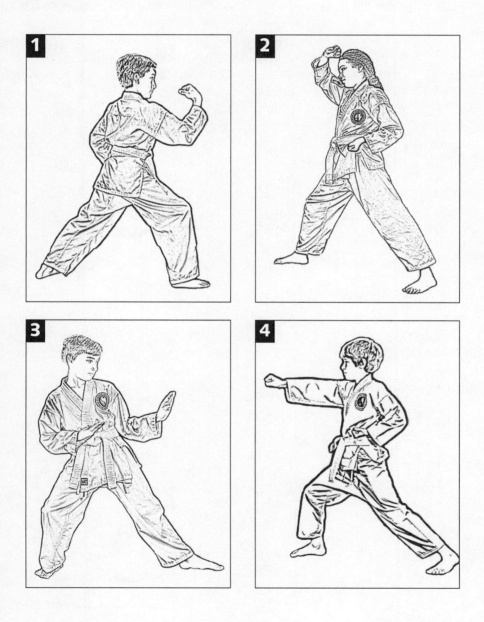

3. Which foot would you use?

For each kick, there's a correct foot to use. Draw a line from the name of the kick to the correct foot. And circle the part of the foot that should strike the target. Hint: One of the kicks has two correct answers.

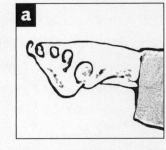

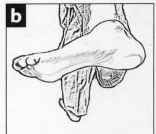

1. Front Snap Kick

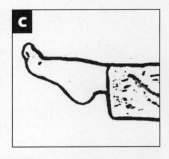

2. Front Thrust Kick

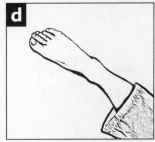

3. Roundhouse Kick

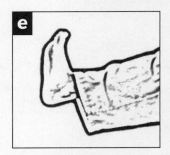

4. Side Thrust Kick

4. Basic training: turn and turn again.

Each time you've learned a new stance, have you tried doing all the different turns in that stance? Back stance and diagonal stance can be especially challenging (not that cat stance and side stance were easy). In back stance, a common mistake is to throw your weight forward when you turn, instead of keeping it over your back leg. You also have to be careful to end with both feet on the line of attack. (It's the same with side stance.) In diagonal stance, it's easy to accidentally move your foot too far—or not far enough—and end up with your back to your opponent (not very safe!).

If you have some sidewalk chalk and a place where it's okay to draw on the pavement, draw a compass showing north, south, east, and west. Turn to page 98 to review the different turns, especially *which foot moves* (front or back) and *which direction you'll end up facing* (depending where you started). Now try all the turns in back stance, then in diagonal stance. It's best to do this with a friend, so you can help each other see if you're ending in the right position each time.

Try it with cat stance and side stance, too. Then add some techniques to do at the end of each turn, as you did in Level Three.

5. Try this at home: watching TV.

Do you sometimes watch TV? That's probably okay as long as you don't do it *too* much. But if you combine it with training, you'll get more from your TV time. Try this: During a commercial, turn your back to the TV; get in a good, low rectangular stance; and hold it till the commercial is over. If you're in a really good stance, it should be hard to hold your position for a long time. If you can hold it for one commercial, next time try two. Or hold it for the entire commercial break.

When your legs are too tired to do rectangular stance again, use the next commercial to hold yourself up in push-up position. Don't actually *do* push-ups; just hold yourself up on your hands and toes with your back straight, head up, and stomach muscles tight. Don't move until the commercial is over. If that's too easy, try longer and longer times. Remember to keep from sagging!

Next, stand in kicking stance and keep your balance while the commercials are on. Try balancing an object on your knee while you're in kicking stance.

There's no limit to what you can practice during commercials. You can do blocks or strikes while you're in rectangular stance. You can do push-ups, crunches, or stretches. Just be sure you have permission, and be sure you have enough space.

ANSWERS:

Name the technique. The student on the left is doing cat stance. The student on the right is doing diagonal stance. **What's wrong with these pictures?** All these students have a bent wrist when their wrist should be straight and strong. Circle the bent wrists. In number 3 the student also has bad posture (leaning back) and his front knee is too straight for a good back stance. Plus, his knifehands aren't right: The reaction hand is cupped, and the blocking hand has the thumb wrong. Extra credit: Number 2 also has more mistakes: Her reaction hand is sagging and has a bent wrist, too. **Which foot would you use?** (1) c—circle the ball of the foot, (2) e—circle the heel, (3) a—circle the ball of the foot; also d—circle the top of the foot or *instep*. (4) b—circle the knife-edge.

Looking Ahead to Advanced Training

If you've learned all the techniques in this book well enough to practice them on your own, you're off to a good start in the martial arts. Now you have your work cut out for you! It's time to practice, practice, practice. There are three main things you need to do:

1. Keep going to class and practicing whatever your teacher says to practice.

2. Keep reviewing the techniques you've already learned. Every time you review, you'll be reminded of what you can do better. That's what this book is for.

3. Keep looking forward to all the new things you will learn.

There is plenty more to learn. There are lots more stances, blocks, and strikes. There are spinning kicks and flying kicks. There are footwork drills to make you quick and agile. There are exercises to make your body strong. You can also look forward to:

Sparring

Sparring is when you practice fighting. You might call it *pretend fighting*, because unlike real fighting, in sparring you only want to practice your skills and try things out. You don't want to injure your partners, and they don't want to injure you. Usually you wear pads

to keep from hurting your partner or yourself accidentally. You have to follow rules to keep yourself and your partner safe. But you also get to find out what it's like to have someone trying to hit or kick you and what it's like to try to use your kicks, punches, and blocks (safely) against someone else.

Sparring is fun! Some students find it scary at first. But if we all treat each other with respect, everyone ends up having a good time.

Mat Work

Mat work is when you practice things like rolling and falling on pads (mats). Martial artists need to learn about falling, because in a fight they may be knocked down or thrown down—or they may just slip and fall. There are ways to avoid getting seriously hurt when you fall, and it's important to learn them. In some schools and styles you also learn about throwing opponents and pinning them so they can't get up. You have to learn to take falls safely, so you and your partners can practice throwing each other.

Weapons

When you reach a certain level of skill in many schools and styles, you begin to practice with weapons. Often you begin with a long staff *(bo)* or short stick *(tambo)*. As you train with a weapon, you try to make it feel like an extension of your body. Then besides being a fun thing to learn, the weapon begins to teach you more about your body and your basic techniques.

There are other weapons besides short or long staff. You've probably seen *nunchaku* (two sticks connected by a rope or chain), *sai* (a three-pronged metal weapon), *kama* (a sickle with a sharp blade), and sword.

Any kind of weapons practice is serious and potentially dangerous. All weapons should be treated with respect and not played with as though they're toys. Your instructor will only let you practice with weapons if you show you are a serious student.

Competition

Do you know what a tournament is? It's where lots of martial arts students get together to compete against each other in sparring, forms, weapons, and maybe even board breaking. Students come from different schools and sometimes from different parts of the country or the world.

In sparring competition, judges watch the fighters closely to see who scores the most points by striking the opponent with proper techniques. In kata or poomse competition, judges score the competitors according to how graceful, powerful, and accurate they are in their performances.

Competing in a tournament might sound scary: You have to get up in front of judges, and lots of people are watching. You might have to spar with a stranger from a different school. You'll probably feel nervous. But it's great practice. You get to find out how to do your best under pressure. If you're shy about performing in front of people, you especially should go. It will help you see that shyness doesn't have to stop you.

The winners get medals or trophies—but that isn't the best part. The best part is getting to meet new people, see some excellent performances, do your best, and have fun.

Assistant Teaching

Almost any student who reaches a high enough level will be asked to help with teaching a class. It's an honor and a responsibility. It is also an important part of learning. When you teach, you get to share some of the gift your instructors have given to you. At the same time, you have to make sure you really understand what you're trying to teach. You also have to learn to understand and get along with different people. That's a valuable skill for everyone to have.

Maybe some of your instructors are senior students who are assisting with class. Show them the same respect and appreciation you show the highest-ranking teacher. If you're lucky and work hard, some day you will be in their position.

Things to Do

1. What are you looking forward to?

How many of the activities we talked about are things students do at your school? Which one do you think you'll like best (or like least)? On the list below, circle the ones you'll be practicing some-day. Next to each one, write down what you're most excited about and what you're least excited about. If there's an activity we didn't talk about, write it down, too! And if you're already practicing some of these things, write down what you like best and like least about each one. (Later, when some time has passed and you've had more practice, look at your answers again. See if you have changed your mind about anything!)

Sparring

Mat Work

Weapons

Competition

Assistant Teaching

2. The Combination Machine.

A lot of your time in class is spent practicing *combinations*—moving in stances, doing a combination of blocks, strikes, and kicks as you move across the floor. You've been making up your own combina-tions for practicing at home. The "Combination Machine" helps you create endless combinations for your home workouts. It contains all your techniques plus *templates* to fit them into.

Take out a piece of paper and divide it into four columns. Write these words across the top, one for each column:

Stances   **Blocks**   **Strikes**   **Kicks**

Strikes are hand techniques—like punch, chop, or backfist. Now fill the columns with the names of all the stances, blocks, strikes, and kicks you know. Leave room to add new ones as you learn them! These are your *techniques*.

On a second piece of paper write down these sentences—the *templates:*

1. Moving (forward/backward) in _____ stance, _____ (block), _____ (strike).

2. Moving (forward/backward) in _____ stance, _____ (kick), _____ (block), _____ (strike).

3. Moving in _____ (stance), _____ (any technique), then shift to _____ (stance), _____ (any technique).

To make a combination, choose a direction (forward or backward) and fill in the blanks with techniques. Once you get the hang of it, you can make new templates with more options and more techniques. Here's an example that's more advanced:

4. Starting in _____ stance, _____ (block), then shift to _____ stance, _____ (strike), _____ (kick) and land in _____ stance, _____ (strike), _____ (strike).

APPENDIX A:
Tie Your Belt

The Physics of Action and Reaction

Remember "action and reaction," from back on page 71? Every punch, chop, or block has an action hand and a reaction hand, one going out and one pulling back. Both should be equally strong, going in opposite directions.

When Sir Isaac Newton said, "For every action, there is an equal and opposite reaction," he was stating what we now call Newton's Third Law of Motion. He wasn't talking about what happens when a martial artist uses both arms to do a good technique—even though martial arts teachers sometimes talk that way. He was describing what happens when objects interact with each other.

In martial arts, we're very interested in that. For example, what happens when our fist or foot interacts with a target or the heavy bag? According to Newton's Third Law, when we push on the bag, the bag pushes back equally in the opposite direction.

Many of us have experienced this. We've kicked the bag really hard, only to bounce off and fall over backward! It feels as though the bag kicked us back, and according to Newton, that's pretty much what it did.

Other times, we kick the bag and make a dent in it, or we kick the bag and it swings away from us. Each of these possibilities is also in keeping with Newton's law.

To understand which outcome will happen and why, we'd have to know a lot of different things, including how fast and hard we're kicking, how big and heavy we are, how big and heavy the bag is, what it's made of.... We'd need a physics class to figure it all out.

The part that martial artists probably care most about is how fast and hard we're kicking (or striking, or blocking). Martial artists want to learn how to generate the most possible force using the motion of their bodies. Even martial arts that don't use kicks and punches are concerned with generating and using the force of a body in motion.

That's where Newton's Second Law of Motion comes in. He figured out that *force* equals *mass* times *acceleration*. (Acceleration has to do with speed of movement and changes in speed.) Since we want our punch or kick to generate the most possible force, one of the things we should do is give it the most possible *acceleration*. And (here's the best part) that's what we are helping to do when we use our reaction hand when we punch!

Instead of just sending one arm out to punch by itself, we add acceleration by using both sides of the body. In fact, if we're doing a good job, we're actually using our entire body to do the punch, from the soles of our feet on up through the rotation of our hips and out through the arm. *The rotation of the hips is very important.* When the reaction hand pulls back, it adds to the rotation and therefore to the acceleration. We also add acceleration when we twist at the end of the punch (remember how your fist started on your side faceup and ended by twisting facedown?). So even though we use words from Newton's Third Law when we describe how to use both arms on a technique, what we're really doing is using Newton's Second Law to make our technique more powerful.

If you want to understand more about Newton's Laws, ask your schoolteacher to recommend some good lessons on physics for your grade level.

The Author in Her Own Words

I started training in the martial arts for the same reason lots of kids start: I saw some friends practicing their kicks, and I wanted to try it, too. They asked their teacher's permission to invite me to class. I went, and that was it—I was hooked! The art was taekwondo, and I loved kicking so much, I practiced till my legs were really sore.

Not long after, our teacher moved away. My friend and I found another school; this time it was a style of karate. They had different forms and different belt colors, but the moves were almost the same. The instructor, a very tough lady named Pauline Short, pushed us to be our best.

Then something happened that happens to lots of students: I got really busy with schoolwork and felt I didn't have time to do karate. I quit going to class. Looking back, I think what I really needed was to manage my time better. Later when I saw how much I missed practicing, I went back to it—even though I was still really busy!

I moved a couple of times. Each time, I had to look for a new school. That was hard, because I had to leave my friends and take class with strangers who treated me like a beginner all over again. That's what happens. Good manners mean you wear a white belt when you join a new school—to show you're willing to learn from your new teacher. You do it even if you have an advanced belt from somewhere else. It isn't polite to show off what you already know. It wasn't easy, but I'm glad I followed good etiquette. Every time I thought I knew a lot, I found out I had a lot more to learn.

Kicking was always my favorite part of training. I earned a black belt in taekwondo. One day, I saw a demonstration of an art called *aikido*. The instructor was throwing and pinning attackers who were coming at her from all sides—it looked so graceful and powerful.

She had such good posture, and kept her good posture even with attackers all around! It stuck in my mind, the same way seeing my friends kicking had stuck in my mind eleven years earlier. I began to practice aikido. I had enough experience training and teaching in taekwondo so I could begin to learn another art without getting mixed up. (I would never have done this as a beginner. If you want to do a good job at anything, don't try to do two things at once!)

In a way, aikido is how I ended up practicing Cuong Nhu. An old friend heard me talk about aikido, and told me I should try Cuong Nhu. It was perfect for me, because it combined a lot of what I loved about aikido and a lot of what I loved about taekwondo (kicking!). (That doesn't mean it would be perfect for you, by the way. You are a completely different person. If you like what you are practicing now, *that's* what is perfect for you.)

I dedicated myself to Cuong Nhu, and since 1992, I've been teaching it at my dojo. Read more about Cuong Nhu in the next section.

APPENDIX D:

Cuong Nhu Karate and Other Martial Arts

Cuong Nhu, which means "hard and soft," comes from Vietnam. It's really a blend of seven different styles of Asian martial arts. The founder of Cuong Nhu, Ngo Dong, began studying martial arts when he was a child. He studied many different arts with his older brothers. He reached high rank in a style similar to Shotokan karate, Gichin Funakoshi's style, and began teaching that to students in Vietnam. Over time he blended together ideas and techniques that came from everything he had studied.

Goju

Ngo Dong taught more than just techniques. He cared about the proper way of life of *karate-do*. There was a war going on in Vietnam, with lots of hardship and suffering. He taught that martial arts training is about doing your best so you can help other people. It isn't to encourage fighting but to give you the skill and confidence to promote peace in the world. His students put this philosophy into action—for example, by practicing first aid and traveling to remote villages to help out in times of flood and other disasters.

Cuong Nhu, like other blended styles of martial arts (Kajukenbo is another example), encourages students to learn from many different approaches. The art continues to change and grow. But it has firm roots in traditional martial arts. Here are the seven styles that went into making Cuong Nhu, plus a few more—so you can see how many different arts there are, and how much there is to learn!

1. **Shotokan karate:** This is the style Gichin Funakoshi taught. It has its origins in Okinawa, like these other styles of karate: Shorin-ryu, Shito-ryu, Isshinryu, Wado Ryu, Goju Ryu. (Guess what *goju* means? "Hard and soft," just like Cuong Nhu.) *Ryu* means "style."

There are too many different styles to name them all. If yours was left out, write it here:

_____

2. **Judo:** The founder of judo, Jigoro Kano, took certain techniques from *jujitsu*—a Japanese term covering all kinds of hand-to-hand fighting methods—and created a system of mental, physical, and moral training that's effective for self-defense but safe enough to practice as a sport. Modern judo is all about wrestling, throwing, and pinning, by taking advantage of your opponent's movements and weight.

3. **Wing Chun:** This martial art was founded by a Buddhist nun during dangerous times in China. It uses close-in fighting techniques that help a smaller, weaker person defeat a bigger, stronger attacker. Efficiency, rather than strength, is of great importance. You might know Wing Chun as the martial art Bruce Lee studied, before he developed his own system.

4. **Aikido:** This art, developed by Japanese martial arts master Morihei Ueshiba, studies ways to take the energy of an attack—a grab or a strike—and transform it into a throw or pin. In other words, you get your opponent to defeat himself with his own strength! You also learn to move in ways that keep you from getting hurt by an attack.

5. **Boxing:** I bet you already know what boxing is. It's a popular kind of fist fighting. Boxers have excellent footwork and hand techniques.

6. **Vovinam:** This is a name that means "martial arts of Vietnam." Vovinam is known for really cool animal techniques, flying kicks, and dynamic two-person forms, as well as training with weapons—like short sticks, long staff, and spear.

7. **Tai Chi:** Have you ever seen people in the park practicing graceful movements very, very slowly? That's tai chi. It might look slow and soft, but don't be fooled. They are training their bodies

to move correctly and are building energy from within. If they ever have to use their movements in self-defense, they will be very powerful and effective.

Remember how we said, in Chapter One, that the different martial arts are different paths leading up the same mountain? Now you can picture how some of those paths look. They cross each other many times along the way. Whichever path you're taking, enjoy the hike—and most of all, stick with it all the way to the top.

Answer Key to Questions Appearing in the Text

Part I

CHAPTER 3

page 23 **Connect the answers: Respect:** 1-h, 2-c, 3-l, 4-e, 5-i, 6-m, 7-j, 8-b, 9-d, 10-g, 11-f, 12-a, 13-k.

CHAPTER 4

page 25 **Do-gi and dobok:** These are words that mean "uniform"— the clothing in which you practice the *do* or *way* of martial arts.

page 33 **Why do people wear uniforms?** Some possible answers include: to show which team they're on (football); to identify themselves so people can find them when they're needed (nurses and police officers); to show discipline within a group (military, police, martial arts); because they're suitable clothes for their kind of work (sports and workout clothes, martial arts, astronauts, car mechanics); and for tradition (martial arts and dance troupes). Add your own answers and examples.

CHAPTER 5

page 36 **Reasons for the bowing-in ceremony:** To show respect for tradition, for what you're practicing and for each other.

CHAPTER 6

page 46 **Reasons to stretch:** To get ready for action, hold each stretch for a count of eight. To increase flexibility, hold each stretch for thirty seconds and repeat it three times.

Part II

LEVEL ONE

page 69 **Rising block:** What's wrong with the two pictures? In one, the roof isn't covering the head—it's off to one side. In the other, it's too flat and too close to the head.

LEVEL TWO

page 83 **When to use a roundhouse knee kick:** One answer would be when your attacker is off to the side, instead of right in front of you.

page 87 **First thumb escape:** What's the weakest part of a wrist grab? It's where the thumb is. The thumb is holding on all by itself, unlike the four fingers, which are supporting each other.

page 88 **Tips on first thumb escape:** If the attacker grabs your left wrist with grab #1, step forward and left with your left foot at the same time you snap your wrist free. Which knee? Your back knee—it's stronger and it's the one that's already in front of your attacker. What kind of knee kick works best? If you moved far forward on your step, you'll probably need to do a roundhouse knee kick, but it really depends where you and your opponent are standing in relation to one another.

LEVEL THREE

page 104 **Second thumb escape:** Grab #2 is opposite-side or cross-hand grab. The side you step to is called the *dead side*. In the first thumb escape the escaping movement was like getting ready to do inner chop.

LEVEL FOUR

page 115 **Before practicing with a partner,** you must always bow to each other. It means you'll treat each other with respect.

page 120 **Blocks & Punches:** His left fist should be at his right ear, palm side facing the ear.

page 122 **Double inner middle block:** Japanese: *morote uchi ude-uke;* Korean: *du backat jung dan makgi.* The starting position is the same as for inner middle block.

page 125 **Third thumb escape** uses grab #3: two hands on two. Does it matter which side you step to? No, you may go to either side, unless there's something in the way or a special reason why one direction is better (maybe it's closer to someone who can help you after you escape). If you step to the left, both hands go to the *right.*

page 126 **Fourth thumb escape:** Grab #4 is two hands on one. Since both thumbs are on top, your arm will have to go upward in order to break out against the thumbs.

LEVEL FIVE

page 132 **Cat stance:** Why is it handy to be able to lift your front foot easily? One good reason is you can kick quickly in self-defense without having to shift your weight first.

page 133 **Side stance:** *kiba dachi, juchŭm sogi.*

page 133–34 **Vertical punch:** Horizontal means "side to side" (along the horizon). Vertical means "straight up" or "up and down." Vertical chop is called vertical because it starts *up* and strikes *down* (vertically). Double vertical punch would be two vertical punches at the same time, like double punch on page 122 but with vertical fists.

page 135 **Vertical backfist** is called "vertical" because it strikes downward, like vertical chop.

page 135 **Outer middle block** is called "outer" because it starts on the outside. The starting position is very similar to outer chop, with the elbow raised up and back, head-level. Both techniques then snap forward and across the body.

page 137 **Blocks & Punches:** The left arm blocks first. The order of blocks is (1) lower block, (2) middle block, and (3) rising block. Do you have to use reaction hand on all blocks? Yes.

True or false: false—the correct answer is left, right, right, left.

page 138 **Fifth thumb escape:** In grab #5, your attacker is behind you.

What else can you do after breaking free? Run away!

LEVEL SIX

page 152 **Knifehand block.** What will the other hand do when one hand does the block? It's the *reaction hand.* It will pull back to your side!

page 156 **Escaping techniques.** Three choke escapes are (1) ducking out, (2) windmill, and (3) double rising block. Our five escapes from wrist grabs are called thumb escapes.

Quick Guide to Techniques, Exercises, and Concepts

Stances

Hand Techniques

Strikes

Escaping Principles and Techniques

Form—Kata—Poomse

Exercises and Drills

Concepts

Notes from Class